There are a number of HORIZON CARAVEL BOOKS
published each year. Titles now available are:

American Heritage also publishes AMERICAN HERITAGE JUNIOR LIBRARY
books, a similar series on American history. The titles now available are:

A HORIZON CARAVEL BOOK

LEONARDO DA VINCI

By the Editors of
HORIZON MAGAZINE

Author
JAY WILLIAMS

Consultant
BATES LOWRY

Professor of Art History, Brown University

ILLUSTRATED WITH THE PAINTINGS, DRAWINGS,
AND DIAGRAMS OF LEONARDO DA VINCI

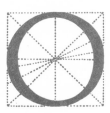

Published by American Heritage Publishing Co., Inc.
Book Trade and Institutional Distribution by
Harper & Row

SECOND EDITION
Library of Congress Catalog Card Number: 65–20599
© 1965 by American Heritage Publishing Co., Inc., 551 Fifth Avenue, New York, New
York, 10017. All rights reserved under Berne and Pan-American Copyright Conventions.
Trademark CARAVEL registered United States Patent Office

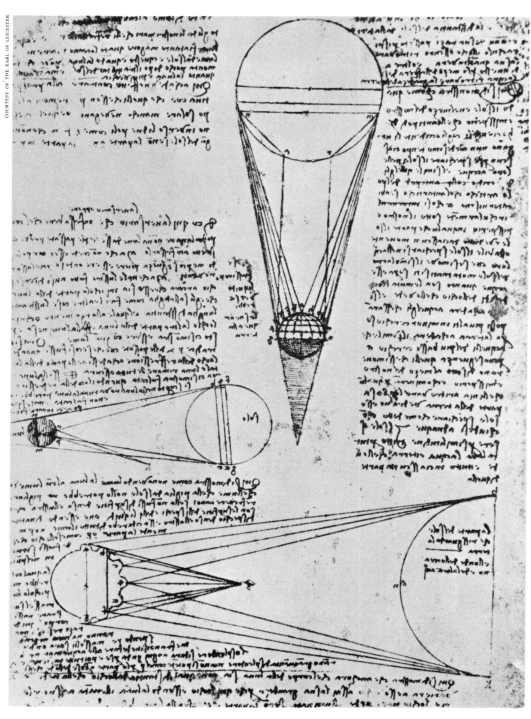

In his day, Leonardo was known only as an artist, yet most of his life was dedicated to the scientific exploration of nature. He was equally at home devising a method of gauging the sun's distance from the earth (above) or charting the anatomy of man in drawings like the study of a heart opposite.

FOREWORD

In his youth Leonardo da Vinci wrote confidently, "I wish to work miracles." By the time of his death in 1519, when he was sixty-seven and famed throughout Europe, it seemed that he had accomplished wonders aplenty. He had gone from a humble village in northern Italy to the palaces of princes, popes, and kings; he had opened up a new world of beauty to future generations of artists by showing them how to paint the inner truth of their subjects; and he had devoted himself to the many branches of science so intensively that even today it is still debated whether he was greater as an engineer, anatomist, or naturalist.

The highest ideal of the remarkable age in which he lived—the Renaissance—was to be a universal man, capable of any adventure, be it military, courtly, or intellectual. Leonardo was that supremely versatile man. But he died unhappy, believing that he had accomplished nothing.

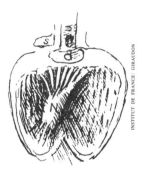

Within the pages of this book are reproduced all of his uncontested paintings, many of his major inventions, and numerous scientific drawings. It is an eye-opening collection, one that makes the viewer see people and animals and all things with sharpened perception. But, as Leonardo himself wondered, why is there so much that is incomplete, why are there so few machines that really work?

Perhaps the explanation lies in a special kind of discontent that was Leonardo's. This is hinted at in the words of his contemporary biographer, Giorgio Vasari: "His knowledge of art, indeed, prevented him from finishing many things which he had begun, for he felt that his hand would be unable to realize the perfect creations of his imagination . . ."

It is indeed Leonardo's mind and spirit that are to be remembered even more than his masterpieces and inventions. Though not the miracle worker he hoped to be, his far-ranging genius gave Western civilization a new look—and a new life.

THE EDITORS

Many of Leonardo's projects, such as this graceful domed church, remained buried in his sketchbooks; never to be tested or constructed.

COVER: *Leonardo was as accomplished a draftsman as he was a painter. This magnificent head of a warrior may be a self-portrait.*

ENDSHEETS: *Leonardo's "Last Supper," his largest painting, and one of his greatest, marked a turning point in the history of art.*

TITLE PAGE: *This "O" and chapter initials on other pages are believed to have been designed by Leonardo for a book on proportion.*

CONTENTS

I APPRENTICE

A new spirit dawned over plague-ravaged and war-racked Europe in the fifteenth century. It was like the opening of a vast door, flooding the lands with light. New concepts of freedom were uttered, new ways of looking at nature appeared. It seemed to many that all things were possible, that reason and knowledge would liberate the minds of men and that the boundless secrets of the universe could be discovered.

At the height of this age of discovery, in 1452, Leonardo was born. He was to sum up in his person the restless genius of the time—to be a painter, inventor, engineer, philosopher, and scientist. Yet his own personality was to remain, to this day, a mystery and an intriguing puzzle.

His beginning was in commonplace surroundings, a background that gave little promise for either art or profound thought. He was the son of Piero, a notary from the village of Vinci, near Florence, from which the family took its name. Piero, an energetic, shrewd, and thrifty man, handled the legal business of the neighborhood with skill, and he had many contacts with the nearby city of Florence, where he had friends among the merchants, craftsmen, and artists. When the peasants of Vinci met him in the streets, they addressed him as "Ser," or "Master," as a mark of respect.

When Piero was a young man in his twenties, his family

Fifteenth-century Florence, although one of the wealthiest and most cultured cities in Italy, still maintained many of the cruel customs of the Middle Ages, such as the burning of heretics (left) in the main square.

had found a suitable bride for him—a girl named Albiera di Giovanni Amadori, who was generally considered to be a good match. Their home was a happy one, although no children were born of the marriage. However, one child grew up in Piero's house—a boy, Leonardo, fathered by Piero before his marriage to Albiera. Young Leonardo was cared for with affection and even had fond uncles who found time to play with him. Yet, as he grew older, Leonardo began to feel that he was different from the people who surrounded him, not merely because he was a stepchild but because he was possessed by a burning curiosity to know everything.

Quickly he absorbed all that his schoolmaster could teach him; impatiently he dropped each new subject after mastering its rudiments and went on to the next. In later life he came to regret this headlong approach, which resulted in a notable lack of formal education.

Much of Leonardo's time was spent roving and exploring the surrounding countryside. The village of Vinci perched on the slopes of Mount Albano. On one side was the fertile valley of Lucca, with its olive trees, orchards, and rich fields, on the other the ragged mountain range where swift streams carved the rocks into strange shapes. "Having wandered for some distance among the overhanging rocks," Leonardo once wrote, ". . . I came to the mouth

The solitary wanderings of Leonardo must have taken him to the Arno Valley (above), which he sketched in 1473. He dated the drawing in the strange mirror writing (upper left) he used for his notes. His rambles were also recorded in nature drawings such as the accurate study of a dragonfly at left.

of a huge cavern before which for a time I remained stupe-
fied . . . my back bent to an arch, my left hand clutching my
knee, while with the right I shaded my eyes; and I bent first
one way and then another in order to see whether I could
make out anything inside, though this was almost impossible because of the intense darkness within. And after
remaining there for a time, suddenly there were awakened
in me two emotions, fear and desire: fear of the dark, threat-
ening cavern, and desire to see whether there might be any
marvellous thing in it." For the rest of his life, Leonardo

13

The artists, artisans, and merchants of Florence were banded into organizations called guilds, each with its own rules, traditions, and symbols. This ceramic plaque displays the sign of the wool merchants' guild.

Parades, pageants, and tournaments served to entertain the wealthy Florentine aristocrats. Above, two bands of gaudily equipped noblemen, crowded

14

was to be driven by this desire to see the marvellous things around him and to discover their meaning.

As a child he kept in his room a collection of things that pleased or interested him, not so different from the collection of any curious boy: snakeskins, odd stones polished by water, birds' eggs, the skeletons of small animals, insects stuck on pins, tadpoles, and strange plants. He discouraged people from entering his room—but in the circumstances, few wanted to. What he could not carry home from his wanderings, he drew on the spot. He must have made countless sketches of the things that littered his room, for at last, Master Piero, looking carefully over his son's work, began to wonder whether the boy might not make a profession of art.

One day, therefore, when Leonardo was fourteen or fifteen years old, Piero took an important step. His business often made it necessary for him to go to the city of Florence, and on one occasion he carried with him a

behind wooden barriers in the square of Santa Croce, joust for the amusement of the ladies in the windows and the commoners jostling at the fence.

15

The workshops of artists and craftsmen were usually found together, lining streets such as the one shown above. Here, clockwise from lower left, are the studios of an armorer, a clockmaker, a scribe, a painter working on an altarpiece, a sculptor, and a designer of musical instruments. A pair of cooks at center are preparing food for the banquet under the arch at top.

portfolio of his son's drawings. He went to the studio of his friend Andrea del Verrocchio to ask his opinion of young Leonardo's work.

Verrocchio was one of the best known artists of Florence. Originally, he had made a reputation as a goldsmith, but he was also recognized as a master sculptor and a highly competent painter. After spending some time in Rome working for Pope Sixtus IV, he had returned to Florence with money in his purse to set up a studio and a school.

Verrocchio saw at once that Leonardo's drawings had more than mere promise. It was arranged that Leonardo would move to the city to begin his apprenticeship.

A boy who wanted to become an artist and a member of the artists' guild, which was similar to a trade union, had to undergo a long period of training. As an apprentice, he lived in his master's house while he learned the secrets of his trade. In return for his food and lodging and his education, he served his master for a number of years, working at the dull chores around the studio and the workshop until he was skilled enough to assist with his master's commissions.

Verrocchio had several apprentices, many of whom, like Leonardo, achieved great fame. Together, these young men learned to prepare wooden panels for painting, to grind colors by hand from lumps of raw pigment and minerals, to make the varnish that was used to protect the finished paintings—and to sweep the floors and keep the studio tidy. They also practiced with sculptors' chisels and round mallets in wood and stone. They sketched from live models or plaster casts in chalk or in pencils with silver points, and they studied proportion and the newly discovered wonders of perspective. Sometimes they molded figures in clay or wax or practiced drawing the folds of drapery from a model made of wet rags soaked in plaster. Leonardo, always quick and eager to learn, took in everything.

Verrocchio was a popular artist who received a variety of commissions, so Leonardo was given a chance to try his hand in nearly all the branches of his calling. Besides, his master was not only an artist but a skillful engineer with an interest in mathematics, and he passed on his knowledge and interest in these fields to his apprentice. Because of his reputation as an artist and as a mechanic, Verrocchio's studio was always a busy and challenging place of work. One week the studio might be casting a bronze candelabrum; the next, making a bas-relief for an altar; and then

Andrea del Verrocchio (1435–1488), Leonardo's master for six years, was as familiar with a mathematician's drafting tools (below) as he was with brushes and chisels.

Leonardo helped his master, Verrocchio, to finish "The Baptism of Christ" (opposite). His contribution, the angel at far left and the background, is the first painting that can definitely be assigned to him. The detail at right shows the contrast in the two styles. Verrocchio's angel has an earthy, urchinlike appeal; Leonardo's angel is an attempt to portray the ideal beauty of a heavenly being, the beginning of the search for perfection that lasted the rest of his life.

painting a religious subject for a chapel. Sometimes the work might be pure engineering: on one occasion Verrocchio was given the task of making a gilded copper ball to crown the cupola of the cathedral of Florence, Santa Maria del Fiore. Leonardo later wrote a note reminding himself to "remember the solder material with which the golden ball of Santa Maria was soldered."

When his period of apprenticeship was over in 1472, Leonardo at the age of twenty was registered in the guild of painters of Florence. Now he was a master, with his unpaid days as an apprentice behind him. He was qualified to accept his own commissions, employ his own workmen, and have his own apprentices. For a time, however, Leonardo chose to continue working in Verrocchio's studio as a paid journeyman. Of course, as a full member of the guild, he played a larger part in the studio's work, assisting his master with large scale commissions and with the more difficult areas of paintings, such as backgrounds and even whole figures.

At this time, he co-operated with Verrocchio on a painting of the baptism of Christ. Most of the picture is certainly Verrocchio's, but there are two angels kneeling beside Christ, and one of these, with an upturned face and a faint suggestion of a smile, is Leonardo's. The background is also the work of the young Leonardo. Painted in oil, which was then a new medium in Italy, it is hazy and unclear.

TEXT CONTINUED ON PAGE 22

BEFORE LEONARDO

The fourteen-hundreds, or the Quattrocento as the period was called in Italy, was a time of ferment in politics, in science, and in art; the painters of the time reflected these changes in their work. They set out to explore the world of ideas as the navigators of that age were exploring the globe. New mediums and techniques, such as oil painting and the study of perspective, provided them with the tools they needed. They broke away from the cramped, narrow tradition of their predecessors, the medieval artists who had labored for the glory

of God and his Church. The Quattrocento artists rejoiced in portraying the glory of God's creation—man—and the world he was learning to control. Two of the masters of the Quattrocento were monks: the gentle, holy Dominican Fra Angelico (1387–1455), so named because it was said that he painted like an angel, and the rowdy, earthly Carmelite Fra Filippo Lippi (1406–1469), who kidnapped a nun and married her. Both men worked on "The Adoration of the Kings," below at left. It is a typical painting of the time, combining the old and the new: though it is crowded with real, lively figures, it also has the bright, simple colors, the lack of perspective, and the unrealistic landscape that marked the work of medieval painters. By contrast, "The Birth of the Virgin" (below), by Domenico Ghirlandaio (1449–1494), is the work of a late Quattrocento master who stands nearer to Leonardo in time and spirit. Both of these great Italian artists shared an interest in the search for classical beauty (note the Roman-style decoration of the room) and in the science of perspective.

21

TEXT CONTINUED FROM PAGE 19

There are no hard, outlined forms. They are instead solid and three-dimensional, and the hills, rocks, and trees in the distance appear blurred, as they would when viewed from afar by the naked eye. This realistic approach was a break away from the traditionally stiff and unnatural backgrounds of earlier painters.

According to a contemporary biographer of Leonardo, the historian Giorgio Vasari, Verrocchio threw down his brush in despair and never painted again when he saw the finished work of his pupil. Whether this story is true or not, Leonardo took over more and more of the painting while Verrocchio concentrated on sculpture, which he seemed to prefer. Soon after working on the painting of Christ's baptism, Leonardo completed an even larger painting, "The Annunciation," which seems to be mostly his own work. The figures of the Virgin and the angel are certainly

TEXT CONTINUED ON PAGE 26

MUSEO NAZIONALE, FLORENCE: ALINARI

The Palazzo Vecchio, the city hall of Florence and focus of much of the city's war-torn history, is at center in the photograph at right. The galleries in the foreground, part of the Uffizi Palace, were designed by Giorgio Vasari, the earliest of Leonardo's biographers. According to some experts, the earliest portrait of Leonardo is the statue of David at left, which was made in 1476 by Verrocchio.

23

"The Annunciation" is Leonardo's first completed painting. It was probably finished in spare moments over a period of years and is typical of the kind of work that artists kept on hand in their studios to display their skill

to possible patrons. Leonardo must have labored on the painting while still in Verrocchio's studio, since the reading stand in front of the Virgin is copied from one designed by his master for a Medici funeral monument.

TEXT CONTINUED FROM PAGE 22

his, as well as part of the background. Although it has a strange perspective and seems the work of a newcomer to painting, "The Annunciation" shows Leonardo's increasing mastery of his craft and hints at the power that was to be fully revealed in his later work.

During this period, when he was in his early twenties, Leonardo also produced other works: a second Annunciation for an altarpiece for the cathedral of Pistoia, just outside Florence, and "The Virgin with the Flowers." He designed a tapestry showing Adam and Eve in a flowery meadow. The final drawing for this, or cartoon, as it is called, was widely admired. At about the same time, he finished a painting of a young Florentine woman, Ginevra de' Benci—his first known portrait (see page 30). As his reputation grew, so did his confidence. At last he bade farewell to Verrocchio and set up his own studio.

A street fight (left) was an everyday sight in fifteenth-century Italy. The unruly princes of the age hired gangs of thugs to settle their differences—they were violent men as well as patrons of art and science. The Medici brothers Giuliano (far left) and Lorenzo (right) were typical of their time, lavishing their wealth on artists and on armies with equal generosity. Giuliano met a bloody end, commemorated in the medallion above, under the daggers of his enemies the Pazzis.

In January, 1478, he received his first commission as an independent artist, an altarpiece for the Chapel of San Bernardo in the Palazzo Vecchio. By March of the same year, he must have been ready to begin painting, since he received an advance on his fee. What subject he chose for the altarpiece is not known, however, for he never finished it. Five years later the work was turned over to Ghirlandaio, a well-established Florentine master, and in 1485 it was replaced with a completely new painting by Filippino Lippi.

No one can say why Leonardo abandoned the altarpiece. Perhaps he was disappointed by his inability to paint what he saw in his mind's eye. His contemporary, the satirist Pietro Aretino wrote, "I say to you that Leonardo was equal to the greatest. His limitation was that he had so elevated a genius that he was never satisfied with what was done." Perhaps, as happened with many of his projects, he lost himself in studying his subject and forgot the original purpose of his research. He was never able to curb his curiosity, even when it interfered with his livelihood. Moreover, his work was continually interrupted by the unsettled conditions in Florence.

Having survived a stormy history, Florence was again being buffeted by civil war. The city had been involved in the struggles between the popes and the Holy Roman Emperors and in conflicts with the rival city-states of Italy in the early 1400's. Finally Cosimo de' Medici, the head of a powerful family of wool merchants and bankers, led the Florentines to victory over the Viscontis of Milan in the Battle of Anghiari in 1440, and an uneasy peace followed. Cosimo became the uncrowned lord of Florence, and after his death his son and then his grandson, Lorenzo the Magnificent, followed in his footsteps. However, Lorenzo quarreled with Pope Sixtus IV over the administration of papal land that had been entrusted to the Medicis. Sixtus, in revenge, turned over the responsibility for his finances to the Pazzis, a rival family of Florentine bankers.

The breach between the Medicis and the pope increased, and in 1478, the quarrel between Lorenzo and the pope flared into violence. One of Sixtus' nephews formed a conspiracy to assassinate Lorenzo and his brother Giuliano at a great religious ceremony the Medici brothers were to attend in April. But the plot was only partially successful. Giuliano was stabbed to death by one of the Pazzis with the aid of a hired assassin, while Lorenzo escaped. The angry Florentines rounded up the conspirators and hanged them from the windows of the council hall. War was now inevitable. Allies of Florence and allies of the pope took up the cause, and for the next six years, Italy was torn by the struggle between them.

Leonardo could not have escaped the disturbing effects of the conflict. Not surprisingly, during this period he began to make the first of his war-machine drawings. Despite his lack of experience in warfare, both his training (which demonstrated that an artist should be able to design anything) and his personal curiosity (which impelled him to study every aspect of life) persuaded him that he could profitably devote his talents to military engineering. Besides, he may have suspected that engineers would be more in demand than artists—even though he hated war and was later to call it "beastly madness."

As with many of Leonardo's later inventions, some of these early designs were completely practical, and some

Bernardo Bandini de' Baroncelli was immortalized in this sketch by Leonardo after being hanged for his part in the murder of Giuliano. Political murder often replaced diplomacy in fifteenth-century Italy, and the professional assassin, typically armed with the narrow-bladed stiletto (opposite), was esteemed as a master craftsman.

29

The painting above, Leonardo's first portrait, is almost certainly the portrait of Ginevra de'Benci, a young Florentine lady mentioned in Vasari's Lives of the Artists. The painting, probably commissioned for her wedding in 1474, still shows the influence of Verrocchio's style in the slanted eyes and solemn expression. One clue to the sitter's identity is the juniper tree (ginepro in Italian) behind her head. The bottom of the original has been cut off for some unknown reason, but the missing hands can be reconstructed from Leonardo's silverpoint study at right.

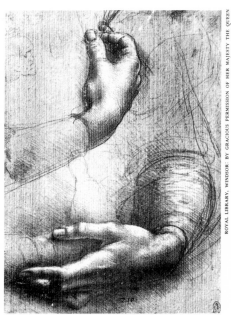

were not, either because they were based on unsound ideas or because they were too advanced to be built by the artisans of his day. A number of his designs, for example, called for some kind of power to drive huge gears—power such as steam, which had not yet been introduced. In any case, the inventor's ingenuity was wasted, since no one seems to have paid any attention to his clever designs.

Finally, in 1480, the war was ended by Lorenzo's skillful diplomacy. And with the return of peace, the Florentines once more turned their minds and their money from fighting to the arts. Proud of the wealth and beauty of their city, they trusted that Florence would continue to dominate the cultural scene in Italy. The city had done so since the early 1400's when the new spirit known as the Renaissance had begun to spread across the land. But the Renaissance was more than its name implied—a rebirth of the artistic principles of ancient Greece and Rome—it was one of the most vital forces that had yet occurred in the development of European civilization. And neither Florence nor any other one city could be expected to possess it entirely. Nor could the new men of this age, remarkably creative "Renaissance" men like Leonardo, be expected to remain at one task or in one city for long.

Early in 1481, Leonardo received his first important commission since the outbreak of the war. The monks of the wealthy monastery of San Donato a Scopeto, just outside Florence, hired him to paint an altarpiece for their high altar. And, remembering the unfinished altarpiece in the Chapel of San Bernardo, they wrote into the contract the stipulation that Leonardo was to complete the work in thirty months at most.

Leonardo set about planning his work with great care. He chose as his subject the Adoration of the Magi, and he made a series of careful drawings, laying out the perspective with mathematical precision. He changed his mind many times, switching the figures and the background around until he had a perfect composition (see page 108). Yet once again he abandoned his painting, leaving it unfinished after seven months' work. The painting contains some sixty-seven figures arranged in an intricate and difficult pattern, and perhaps Leonardo realized that his approach was too ambitious for even his great talent and that he would never make a success of the completed work. Or perhaps a more practical matter interrupted his labors.

Leonardo's reputation in Florence was not entirely due to his skill as a painter or as an engineer. He was also

The Virgin and Child was a subject often painted by Leonardo while he was in Verrocchio's studio. The Madonna above may have been done then; but because it has been badly overpainted, many experts will not ascribe the work to Leonardo. The sketch below of a child with a cat was a study for another Madonna.

well known as a musician. Vasari says, "He gave some time to the study of music and learnt to play on the lute, improvising songs most divinely." This was an important accomplishment in fifteenth-century Italy. Certainly Lorenzo the Magnificent thought so, for he sent Leonardo to Milan to present to its ruler, Lodovico Sforza, a silver lyre in the shape of a horse's skull, which the ingenious artist had made.

Leonardo must have been delighted at the prospect of going to Milan. He no longer felt at home in the fierce, competitive air of Florence where he had found neither fame nor fortune. Besides, Lorenzo the Magnificent had little time for painters; he was more interested in writers. Lodovico Sforza, on the other hand, was a man of wide and varied interests: his court had become a center not only for artists but also for scholars—scientists, mathematicians, doctors, and engineers—from whom Leonardo could hope to learn much.

He must have had little regret when, leaving his unfinished altarpiece behind, he abandoned his studio and packed his belongings, among them many samples of the work he had done in Florence: ". . . certain figures of Saint Jerome . . . drawings of knots . . . some machines for ships [and] for water . . . many heads of old men . . . a madonna, finished . . . another almost, which is in profile."

And so at the age of thirty, Leonardo turned his back on his native city and set out for a new and, he hoped, more rewarding career in Milan.

The silver horse-headed lyre that prompted Leonardo's visit to Milan was probably similar to the instrument above, which he later sketched in his notebook. The unfinished painting of Saint Jerome opposite may have been one of several that were included in his baggage on that fateful journey.

II ARTIST

Lodovico Sforza, known as Il Moro, was one of the greatest patrons of the arts in Italy, but his career as ruler of Milan ended in disaster.

At the beginning of the fourteenth century, Matteo Visconti made himself ruler of Milan, and his heirs ruthlessly extended their power over much of northern Italy. During the first half of the fifteenth century, they fought a series of bitter wars with the Medici family of Florence, which ended with the defeat of the Viscontis at Anghiari.

By 1450, Milan had become a fairly peaceful and stable duchy ruled by Lodovico's father, Francesco Sforza, who had been put in power by the people themselves. Francesco had the wisdom to make alliances with the Medici princes of Florence and with the king of Naples, who ruled most of southern Italy. When Francesco died in 1466, a generation before Leonardo's arrival in Milan, it was with the knowledge that his older son, Galeazzo, was inheriting a secure and prosperous city.

It was as regent for Galeazzo's young son, Gian Galeazzo, that Lodovico came to power in 1476. He was a man of guile and of startling appearance—he was generally called Il Moro ("the Moor") because of his swarthy skin. But as a Renaissance ruler, he carried on the tradition of his father: he encouraged artists and scholars to settle in Milan, and he continued to improve and beautify the city. His court became one of the most brilliant centers of the Renaissance, since with an income of half a million ducats (about $1,125,000) a year he could afford to be lavish.

"He who has the opportunity," wrote Leonardo, "and

The Gothic pinnacles of Milan cathedral (opposite) were unique in Italy, for it was designed by northern architects imported by the Viscontis.

waits for another, loses his friends and never has any money." Leonardo had been provided with the opportunity to go to Milan, and he seized it. He realized, however, that the more versatile and talented the person, the more desirable his presence at a highly accomplished court. Therefore, in a letter to Lodovico he promoted himself unabashedly, enumerating his abilities as an artist, sculptor, and engineer. Since the Italian states were so often at war with one another, he particularly emphasized his military inventions.

His letter catalogued the secret devices that he had invented and which he could provide for Lodovico: portable

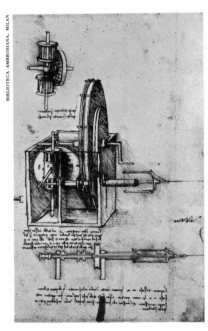

Milan's wealth was based on its textile industry, and during his years in the city, Leonardo invented several new weaving devices, such as the automatic spindle above. The city was also the armor-making center of Europe. The leading family of armorers, the Missaglias, who made the magnificent suit at right, employed hundreds of craftsmen in their mass-production shops.

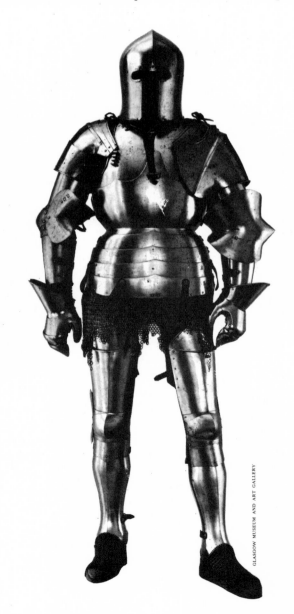

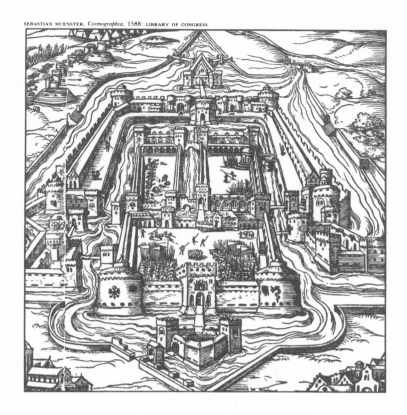

SEBASTIAN MUENSTER, *Cosmographia*, 1588: LIBRARY OF CONGRESS

The stormy history of Milan made a well-fortified home a necessity. The sprawling Castello Sforzesco (left), residence of the Sforzas, was provided with sturdy walls by Lodovico's father. Il Moro spent a fortune beautifying the interior.

bridges, new kinds of mortars, large cannon, and giant catapults; new methods of mining walls during a siege; "covered chariots, safe and unassailable" (forerunner of the tank); and new weapons for naval warfare. Only at the end of his letter did Leonardo mention his skill as an artist. "Also I can execute sculpture in marble, bronze, or clay," he wrote, "and also painting, in which my work will stand comparison with that of anyone else, whoever he may be." His ideas must have impressed Lodovico—or at least interested him—for he soon hired Leonardo. It was an association that lasted until Il Moro fell from power eighteen years later.

During that time, Leonardo was steadily employed by the court in a variety of ways. He cast cannon, as his master, Verrocchio, had done for Lorenzo de' Medici; he designed costumes and stage machinery for pageants; and he supplied advice on all sorts of subjects, mechanical and artistic. But as an unfettered and ambitious newcomer to Milan, he was also ready and willing to take on whatever other challenges the city might have to offer.

TEXT CONTINUED ON PAGE 40

REPUBLIC OF

Trent

Feltre

Lake
Como

Asolo

COLLEONI

Bergamo

Vicenza

Venice

Verona

Padua

Brescia

Lake
Garda

Chioggia

LOMBARDY

MINCIO RIVER

ADIGE RIVER

Milan

Lodi

SFORZA   VISCONTI

Pavia

GONZAGA   Mantua

Cremona

MANTUA

Ferrara

PO RIVER

Mirandola

D'ESTE

FERRARA

Parma

DUCHY OF
MILAN

Fornovo

Modena

BENTIVOGLIO

Bologna

Imola

Faenza

Forlì

DUCHY
OF
MODENA

Pistoia

Genoa

Sarzana

REPUBLIC OF
GENOA

Carrara

REPUBLIC
OF LUCCA

Prato

Fiesole

Florence

MEDICI

Lucca

REPUBLIC OF
FLORENCE

GULF OF
GENOA

Pisa

ARNO RIVER

TUSCANY

PETRUCCI

Livorno

Volterra

Siena

REPUBLIC
OF
SIENA

ELBA

CORSICA

d Greenspan

RENAISSANCE ITALY

Fifteenth-century Italy was a tangle of small independent states. The kings of Naples controlled the south; the popes, temporal as well as spiritual leaders, ruled the center; and a pack of princelings and city-republics fought for supremacy in the north. The chief contenders were Florence, Milan (the gateway to Italy), and Venice (the mistress of the Adriatic Sea). Despite their unending quarrels, these cities were the source of that incredible upheaval in society, philosophy, and the arts called the Renaissance, which was to be the setting for the unique genius of Leonardo da Vinci.

VENICE

Trieste

Ravenna

ROMAGNA

Cesena

Rimini

MALATESTA

Pesaro

Fano

San Marino

Sinigaglia

Borgo
San Sepolcro

Urbino

Ancona

MONTEFELTRO

THE
MARCHES

Anghiari

Arezzo

BAGLIONI

Perugia

Assisi

STATES OF
THE CHURCH

ADRIATIC SEA

Lake
Trasimeno

Pienza

Orvieto

Lake
Bolsena

Viterbo

TIBER RIVER

Aquila

Tivoli

KINGDOM OF
NAPLES

Rome

COLONNA

THE PAPACY

URSINI

Ostia

Benevento

TYRRHENIAN SEA

ARAGON

Naples

Am

ISCHIA

A wedding banquet similar to the feast shown in the fresco at left celebrated the marriage of Gian Galeazzo Sforza and Isabella of Aragon. Leonardo designed an elegant pageant for the festivities.

TEXT CONTINUED FROM PAGE 37

Soon after his arrival in Milan, Leonardo came into contact with a family of hard-working craftsmen named de Predis. Through them he received his first important contract in the city, a huge altarpiece for the Church of San Francesco Grande.

The Confraternity of the Immaculate Conception, a religious society that drew its members from among the best families in Milan, had ordered the altarpiece two years before. Evangelisto de Predis had been busy carving the massive frame. Now it was ready for gilding, and the three panels were to be painted. The confraternity had described in the contract exactly what they wanted: a painting of the Virgin and Child with two prophets in the center panel, which was Leonardo's share of the work, and singing angels on the side panels, which were to be done by Ambrogio de Predis.

Renaissance artists rarely felt obliged to follow the wishes of their employers down to the last detail, and the painting that Leonardo provided for the confraternity was quite different from what they had ordered. He felt, perhaps, that their price of one hundred ducats was too low for a completely new painting, so he offered them instead a copy of a work that he had brought from Florence—his own "Virgin of the Rocks." The subject was a meeting between the Christ Child and the infant Saint John the Baptist. Yet, curiously, though the two paintings are of the same subject and by the same artist, there are several small and striking differences. Fortunately, for the sake of comparison, both paintings have survived in good condition. The Florence "Virgin of the Rocks" is in the Louvre in Paris, and the confraternity's version is in the National Gallery in London (see overleaf).

In both the seated Virgin stretches a protective hand over her Son, who sits at her feet with one hand raised in blessing. Beside the Virgin kneels the infant Saint John. There are no prophets and only one angel. In the original version of the painting, the angel looks out at the viewer with a mysterious half-smile and points a long, elegant finger toward Saint John. The angel's face seems to have been an ideal of beauty for Leonardo, for he drew similar faces over and over again. And the half-smile and pointing finger must have had a special meaning for the artist because he used them many times in his sketches and paintings. But what they signified remains a mystery, although scholars and critics have long tried to unravel the riddle.

In the confraternity's painting, Leonardo changed the angel slightly. The mysterious pointing finger has disappeared, and the angel's eyes look directly at Saint John.

The setting is a brooding landscape of rocks that arches over the figures like the roof of a cave. Perhaps the scene grew out of a memory of his childhood wanderings among the rocky hills around Vinci. In his notebooks Leonardo recalled the feeling of awe and terror that overcame him when he found his way into a cavern, and perhaps he was trying to suggest these feelings in the paintings.

According to the contract, the altarpiece was to have been finished by December, 1483. However, the work was not completed because a dispute broke out over money. Apparently both the de Predis family and Leonardo demanded to be paid more than the contract had originally granted them; they pointed out that the contract also allowed them to ask for more funds. Eventually Leonardo was able to obtain another twenty-five ducats for his part of the work. But the altarpiece, for all the moody beauty of its central panel, remained unfinished.

In the years that followed, Leonardo made every effort to show by his competence as a court artist—and his ability to create anything—that he was ready for whatever greater commission Il Moro might conceive. He painted portraits of members of the court, including Lodovico's mistress, Cecilia Gallerani. His painting of her is known as "The Lady with an Ermine" because Cecilia is holding an er-

TEXT CONTINUED ON PAGE 45

Many religious societies and confraternities performed charitable work and took part in religious festivals such as the procession of Corpus Domini above. They were also among the most generous patrons of art in the Renaissance.

Leonardo made two versions of "The Virgin of the Rocks." The earlier of the two (above), probably completed before he left Florence, is in the Louvre Museum in Paris; the second copy, which is believed to be the altarpiece ordered by the confraternity in Milan, is in the National Gallery in London. These paintings marked a historic advance in the history of art, for, in contrast to earlier painters, who separated shapes by

outlining them, Leonardo modeled his figures with light and shadow alone. This technique, which is called chiaroscuro, gave them a solid, three-dimensional appearance. He also grouped his figures into a pyramid, so that the eye is drawn naturally to the main point of interest, the Virgin's head. Leonardo developed and perfected both of these techniques, which became basic laws for succeeding generations of artists.

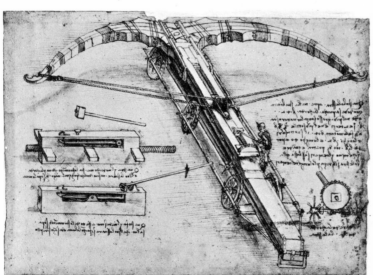

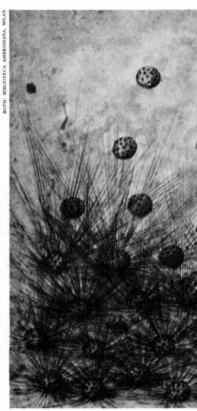

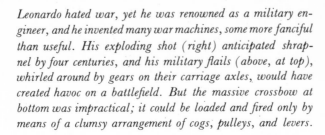

Leonardo hated war, yet he was renowned as a military engineer, and he invented many war machines, some more fanciful than useful. His exploding shot (right) anticipated shrapnel by four centuries, and his military flails (above, at top), whirled around by gears on their carriage axles, would have created havoc on a battlefield. But the massive crossbow at bottom was impractical; it could be loaded and fired only by means of a clumsy arrangement of cogs, pulleys, and levers.

TEXT CONTINUED FROM PAGE 41

mine (see page 49). Lodovico also made use of Leonardo's talents as an engineer. The artist's notebooks at this time are filled with architectural studies, war machines, and inventions. Among other things, he built an air-cooling machine for Lodovico's wife, Beatrice d'Este. This was a huge water wheel that worked a bellows, sending cooling wafts of air through the lady's suite.

Another of Leonardo's duties was to design the masques, or musical pageants, that were an important part of the life of the court. In February, 1489, Isabella of Aragon, the granddaughter of the king of Naples, came to Milan to marry Lodovico's nephew, Duke Gian Galeazzo. The city was hung with tapestries and wreaths, and elaborate festivities were planned to celebrate the wedding. Even the cooks and servants, wrote the Florentine ambassador, were going about in silks and satins. Leonardo was commissioned to decorate the courtyard of the ducal palace. He built a colonnade with pillars of twigs and a

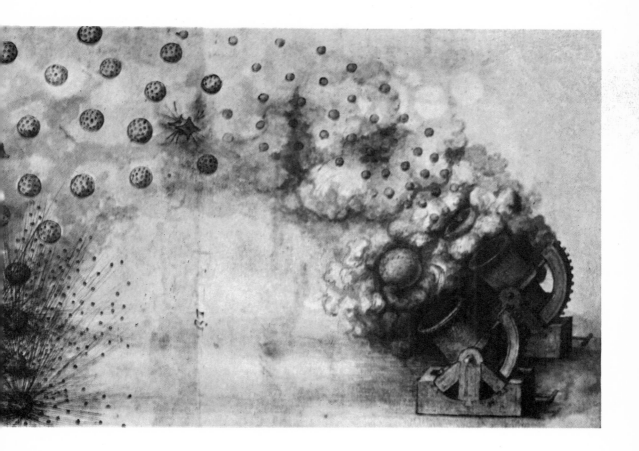

R. de franza

Renaissance rulers surrounded themselves with the pageantry and pomp that befitted their proud station. At left, Charles VIII of France, crowned, robed, and riding a spirited charger, enters a conquered city in the style of an Eastern potentate under a canopy held by eight defeated noblemen.

roof of leaves so tightly woven and trimmed that they looked more like a painting than the real thing. He was also responsible for the masque with which the guests were entertained after the wedding. It was called *il Paradiso,* "Paradise." The audience was amazed by the spectacle. There were Scythians and Moors in dazzling golden cloaks who rode into the great hall among the dancers to offer homage to the bride. And when the curtain across one end of the hall was raised, the guests burst into cries of astonishment. Before their eyes was spread the dome of heaven, glittering with stars, twinkling with the planets and the signs of the zodiac. The planets moved, and the ancient gods after whom they were named—Jupiter, Mars, Venus —came flying from the sky in full costume while hidden choirs sang the praises of the young duke and his wife. The costumes and the machinery that sent the gods soaring and kept the stars twinkling were all Leonardo's work.

However, his most important commission was an equestrian monument to Lodovico's father, Francesco, showing him mounted and armed for battle. Lodovico had planned this for some time, and Leonardo had mentioned it in his first letter to him: "Again, the bronze horse may be taken in hand, which is to be to the immortal glory and eternal honor of the prince your father . . ."

One of Verrocchio's most famous works was a bronze equestrian statue of another notable warrior, Bartolommeo

Colleoni, but Leonardo planned to outclass his teacher. He proposed to make the horse almost twenty-four feet high and to cast it in once piece from 160,000 pounds of metal. Such a task would be difficult even today, but Leonardo was never one to think small.

Leonardo's main problem was to bring to life a mettlesome, fiery animal that would symbolize pride and power. Characteristically, he plunged into the study of horses with great energy. He drew dozens of sketches, spent long hours at the stables of various noblemen, and recorded horses that might be useful as models: "The Sicilian [horse] of Messer Galeazzo . . . Big horse of Cermonino belongs to Signor Giulio . . . White stallion belonging to the falconer

The bustling merchants of Italy were too busy with their trading to bother with war. They hired companies of mercenary troops, led by captains called condottieri, to do their fighting for them. One of the greatest condottieri was Bartolommeo Colleoni (1400–1475), who was commemorated by the grateful people of Venice in this magnificent bronze statue designed by Verrocchio.

The Sforzas recorded their history in a lavishly illustrated book with portraits of the first four dukes of Milan on the opening page (opposite): Franceso, founder of the family fortune, appears in a panel set into the text; Galeazzo is in the upper right margin; and his son, Gian Galeazzo, is kneeling with Lodovico (right) at bottom. The mulberry tree in the lower right margin was a family badge. Lodovico's personal emblem, an ermine, appears in the portrait of his mistress, Cecilia Gallerani, at right, painted by Leonardo around 1481.

has fine haunches . . . The Florentine morel of Messer Mariolo, a big horse, had a fine neck and a very fine head.''

He also designed special molds for the bronze casting and made special furnaces—four of them—in which the bronze would be melted. By autumn, 1493, he had finished a full-scale model of the horse in clay. It was set up in one of the courtyards of the palace in Milan, and everyone who saw it admired it. One distinguished visitor wrote that if Master Leonardo had done no other work in Milan, this alone would have made him famous. But once again, he was not to finish a project. The world and its unrest came between him and his work.

Lodovico's ambition had always been to make himself duke in place of his weak nephew, Gian Galeazzo, but he feared objections from the king of Naples if he should take the ducal coronet. So Il Moro turned to the king of France, Charles VIII, inviting him to acquire the crown of Naples, thus removing the threat posed by that southern kingdom. Through his agents, Lodovico urged the twenty-four-year-old Charles to assert his ancestral rights to Naples. And in September, 1494, Charles crossed into Italy with a well-trained and well-supplied force of some fifty thousand soldiers.

The northern cities, unable to defend themselves, wisely chose to open their gates in welcome. Charles, riding his great black charger Savoia under a golden canopy, entered each new town in full triumph, as if a great military victory had been won. Meanwhile, young Gian Galeazzo fell mysteriously ill, and rather conveniently for his uncle, died in late October. When the ruthless Il Moro heard the news,

Charles VIII (kneeling above), at the height of his triumph, received a golden rose from Pope Alexander VI as a token of victory. Yet within a year, the French king had to fight his way home through the combined armies of the pope and his Italian allies. In the illustration of the Battle of Fornovo at right, Charles (in a crowned helmet at far right) breaks through the allied line with a series of furious charges, finally opening the road to safety.

he immediately summoned the Grand Council. Before morning, the bells of Milan were ringing in honor of the new duke, Lodovico Sforza.

King Charles continued his victorious procession. At Florence, Piero de' Medici, the vain and cowardly son of Lorenzo the Magnificent, rushed to the French camp to sign a treaty of friendship with Charles. Infuriated by Piero's deceit, the people of Florence rose against him, and he and his brothers were forced to flee from the city. With the Medicis' departure, Florence once more became a republic.

In Milan, Il Moro was much pleased with these good tidings. He heard with satisfaction that his ally King Charles had entered Naples and seized the crown without a drop of blood being shed. Now it remained only to get rid of Charles, and Lodovico would be supreme in Italy. The opportunity for that characteristic bit of treachery came when Spain and Germany formed a league with

TEXT CONTINUED ON PAGE 54

A. VERARD, *Mer des Histoires*, PARIS, C. 1503

"*The Last Supper*" *is considered by many to be Leonardo's greatest painting; it was done after peace had once again come to Renaissance Italy with the expulsion of Charles' forces and the momentary triumph of Lodovico Sforza. Artists before Leonardo had tried to recreate this dramatic moment in the life of Christ, but no one had succeeded in portraying it with such nobility and force. The Apostles de-*

picted by Leonardo are individual personalities; their gestures of horror, anger, or despair at Christ's prediction of his betrayal are natural and real. By skillful grouping of his characters, Leonardo has also set off the serene central figure of Jesus, separated from His followers by the foreknowledge of His death, and has emphasized the isolation of Judas, who sits alone and in shadow (the fourth from the left).

TEXT CONTINUED FROM PAGE 51

Venice and the pope to seal off the French in Italy. Quickly, Lodovico threw in his lot with the league and joined the forces arrayed against Charles. Thus, six months after he had entered Naples in an ermine robe, Charles found himself retreating up the Italian peninsula. Only by fighting through the league's superior forces at Fornovo was he able to clear a road back to France for himself and his troops.

But as Il Moro's star rose to its zenith Leonardo found his own prospects becoming no brighter. There was no further talk of the great horse; the bronze collected for it had all been made into cannon. And the duke, occupied with great deeds, seemed to have little time for art—or for the financial needs of his court artist. Leonardo felt compelled to write: ". . . if your Lordship thought that I had money, your Lordship was deceived, because I had to feed six men for thirty-six months, and have had only fifty ducats." It appeared that the duke's treasurer, Gualtieri, had stopped all payments. Leonardo continued: "It may be that your Excellency did not give further orders to Messer Gualtieri, believing I had money."

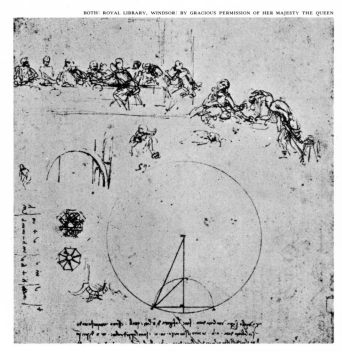

Only at the end of 1495 did Leonardo's fortunes improve. At last Il Moro found a challenging commission for his artist. A wall painting was needed for the dining room of the Convent of Santa Maria delle Grazie. Several years before, the duke had had the artist Montorfano paint the Crucifixion on one end wall of this simple, pleasant room. Now Leonardo was asked to complement it by a painting at the other end. As was the custom, the subject assigned was the Last Supper of Jesus and the Disciples.

For Leonardo this was more than a religious decoration: it was a moment of tense drama, the moment at which Christ revealed to his Disciples that one of them was going to betray Him. The background of "The Last Supper" was to be stark (see pages 52–53); attention was to be focused on the central figure of Christ and on the dramatic emotions of the others. Leonardo had written in his notes on the art of painting: "Make your work in keeping with your purpose and design: that is, when you make your figure you should consider carefully who it is and what you wish it to be doing . . . that figure is most praiseworthy which

When the prior of Santa Maria delle Grazie complained that Leonardo was taking too long over "The Last Supper," the artist replied: "Men of genius really are doing most when they work least, as they are thinking out ideas." He worked on the painting with more than usual care, pondering over it for days at a time and making numerous studies, including the head of Saint James at far left, the trial groupings at left and above, and Saint Peter's arm at right.

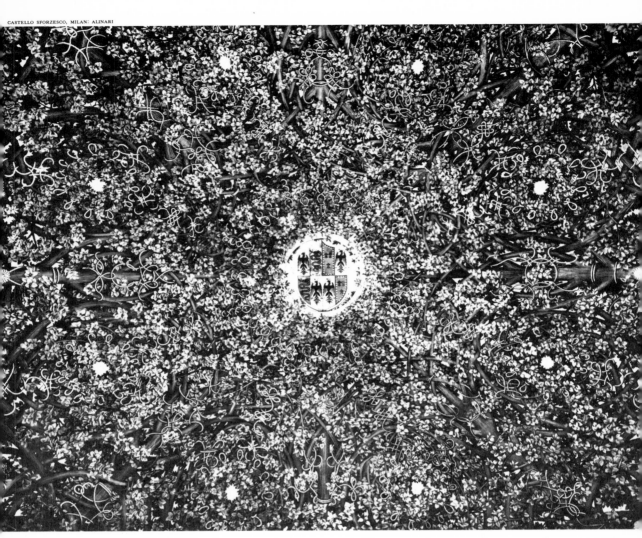

The ceiling of the Paneled Hall (above) is a triumphant display of Leonardo's talent for decoration. His lifelong interest in complicated knots may have stemmed from the fact that vinci, *the Italian word for knots, is a pun on his own name.*

by its actions best expresses the passions of the soul."

After much thought and study Leonardo finally began the painting. Most murals at this time were made by mixing colors with water and applying the mixture to fresh plaster. This kind of wall painting was called a fresco. The work had to be done rapidly since the plaster dried quickly; on the other hand, the colors were bound tightly to the wall and lasted a long time. Leonardo worked very slowly and thoughtfully. In consequence, he decided to use a medium containing oil and tempera so that he could continually retouch, make changes, add little by little to the work, and take his own time about it. He was, apparently, doing some minor jobs on the side for the duke and had

DVODECEDRON PLANV
VACVVS.

Fra Luca Pacioli (c. 1450–1520) was a Franciscan monk and one of the leading mathematicians in Milan. He became Leonardo's friend and teacher, and Leonardo supplied the illustrations, including the geometrical figure at left, for his treatise, Divine Proportion.

not completely given up hope that his horse might still be cast, for he went now and then to do a little more work on it. But most of his concentration was on "The Last Supper," which filled his thoughts night and day. The novelist Bandello has left a description of Leonardo at work:

Many a time I have seen Leonardo go early in the morning to work on the platform before "The Last Supper"; and there he would stay from sunrise till darkness, never laying down the brush but continuing to paint without eating or drinking. Then three or four days would pass without his touching the work, yet each day he would spend several hours examining it and criticizing the figures to himself. I have also seen him, when the fancy took him, leave the [courtyard] where he was at work on the stupendous horse of clay and go straight to the Grazie. There, climbing on the platform, he would take a brush and give a few touches to one of the figures; and then suddenly he would leave and go elsewhere.

Leonardo himself described his working methods: "It is a good plan every now and then to go away and have a little relaxation," he wrote, "for then when you come back to the work, your judgment will be surer . . . It is also advisable to go some distance away [when you look at it] because then the work appears smaller, and more of it is taken in at a glance, and a lack of harmony or proportion in the various parts and in the colors of the objects is more readily seen."

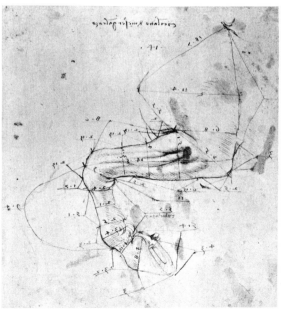

Before commencing work on the Sforza monument, Leonardo carefully studied many horses in the palace stables and elsewhere. He tried to analyze the perfect proportions of a horse in drawings like the one at left, hoping to produce an ideal horse by combining the best features of several different animals. One result of his research is the striking study above. The drawing at right is another of Leonardo's ideas for the finished version of the statue, showing how he altered the rider's gesture for a more pleasing design. The fallen enemy warrior, crouching beneath the flailing forehoofs, acts as an additional support for the statue's massive weight.

The work stretched over a period of three years. At times visitors—perhaps fresh from observing and commenting on the famous horse in the palace courtyard—would come and watch him. For Leonardo did not mind such observation, and in fact, he even " . . . encouraged any beholder to express his thoughts freely."

In such a climate the great painting, with its wonderful faces and passionate gestures, grew to completion. For four and a half centuries it has been considered one of the most profound works of man. Literally millions of words have been written about it by wise or foolish authors; millions of people have seen it in copies or photographs; artists of every period have used it as a model or drawn it for their own pleasure or instruction. Yet most of those who have seen it have actually seen very little of the original. Unfortunately, the wall was damp, and Leonardo's decision to use oil and tempera was a disastrous one.

Soon after it was finished, the painting began to peel off the wall. It has been repainted and restored many times since then, not always to advantage. But there still shines in it a sense of its first magnificence. "A beautiful shadow . . . is all that remains," wrote the American novelist Henry James, "but that shadow is the artist's thought."

III ENGINEER

In the spring of 1499, Leonardo seemed to burst free from his troubles into a clear patch of sunlight. To make up for his unpaid salary, he was given a pleasant vineyard outside Milan by the expansive duke, Il Moro. The gnarled vines on his hillside may have reminded him of the wonderfully intricate design that he had recently wrought for the ceiling of a great room, the Paneled Hall, in the Sforza palace.

Happily Leonardo noted in his account book: "I found myself with 218 lire on the first of April, 1499." But even more happily, he found that he was in a position to keep on creating—or merely thinking—as he chose. In the summer he again picked up his studies of mechanics and his work in geometry and mathematics. He supplied geometrical drawings for a mathematical treatise, *Divine Proportion*, by his good friend and teacher, Fra Luca Pacioli. And during the same year, the duke also appointed him to the post of engineer.

Leonardo set to work at once inspecting the great stone fortresses that guarded Milan and making some suggestions for strengthening them, for Lodovico was menaced by fresh threats of war. King Charles had died, and the new king of France, Louis XII, was determined to try again to secure the French claim to Naples: he would take Milan and use it as his stronghold in the north. In August, 1499, Louis led his troops into Italy and marched on Milan.

By chance, the city fell without a struggle. Lodovico was in Germany, trying to win the emperor's support against Louis, and in his absence, his enemies in Milan welcomed the invaders. Within three months, Il Moro himself had been captured and shipped off to prison in France,

The bird's-eye-view map of Tuscany at left is typical of all Leonardo's work, combining beauty with accuracy. Made while the artist was Cesare Borgia's chief engineer, it was a forerunner of the modern aerial map.

Raphael

A new generation of artists rose to prominence while Leonardo was away from Florence. Among the leaders were his fellow student Lorenzo di Credi and his bitter enemy Michelangelo. And soon to follow were the "divine" painter Raphael, who came to the city in 1504 and fell under the spell of Leonardo's work, and the sculptor Bandinelli and his pupil Benvenuto Cellini—the incomparable goldsmith whose account of his own scandalous career became a classic of Italian literature. Giorgio Vasari, painter and architect, is better known as a writer: his Lives of the Artists *made him the father of art history and criticism.*

Lorenzo di Credi

while French archers billeted around the Sforza palace used Leonardo's great horse for target practice.

Leonardo's period of happiness had swiftly come to a close. His career in Milan crumbled as he watched helplessly; without hope or purpose he decided to leave the city. In December, 1499, he packed up his things, sold what he could not move, and, in a moment of shrewdness, dispatched his money directly to Florence, where it was to be invested. Then he took to the open road, accompanied by Fra Pacioli, heading for Florence by a roundabout route across northern Italy.

First, Leonardo went to Mantua, where he stayed several months and sketched Isabella d'Este, the brilliant wife of its ruler (see page 64). Then he moved on to Venice, where he received a warm welcome and helped to plan the city's defenses against a threatened invasion by the Turks. Finally, toward the end of April, 1500, he set out for Florence.

He had been away for eighteen years, and there had been many changes. His old master, Verrocchio, was dead; so were the great artists Pollaiuolo and Ghirlandaio. Old friends, fellow apprentices like Lorenzo di Credi and Piero di Cosimo, were masters in their own right, and Perugino,

Giorgio Vasari

Michelangelo

Bandinelli and Cellini

who had starved himself to be able to study with Verrocchio, had become one of Italy's most admired painters. Leonardo, though homeless now and without a patron, felt reasonably confident that among this company he would be recognized as established; to his pleasure and relief, he was greeted as an artist who had brought credit to his native city.

The Servite monks of Florence had commissioned an altarpiece for the high altar of the Church of the Annunciation from Filippino Lippi, the same artist who had been called in before to complete work that Leonardo had left unfinished. According to Vasari, "Leonardo said that he would gladly have undertaken such a work. This was repeated to Filippino, and he, like the good fellow he was, withdrew from the assignment." The monks were delighted with this arrangement and even arranged to lodge Leonardo and his assistants while they were at work.

Leonardo planned to paint the Virgin and Saint Anne with the Infant Jesus. He began with a study in chalk, which, says Vasari, "not only filled all artists with wonder, but when it was finished, men and women, young and old, continued for two days to crowd into the room where it was exhibited . . . and all were astonished at its excellence."

But, unfortunately, this was as far as Leonardo went, and the unhappy monks had to apply to Filippino Lippi to take over the project after all.

Other patrons were also trying—without success—to get Leonardo to paint for them. Although he completed "The Virgin with the Yarn Winder" for the secretary of King Louis of France, he refused to complete the portrait of Isabella d'Este that he had begun in Mantua. Her agent, Fra Pietro da Novellara, had to report that Leonardo was "working hard at geometry and has no patience with his brush . . . his mathematical experiments have so distracted him from painting that the sight of his brush puts him out of temper."

Heedless of his growing reputation as a great artist who did not follow through to the end, Leonardo found himself too busy to paint. He wrote long essays on force and motion and made magnifying lenses with which he studied the moon. He experimented with falling objects and concluded that "every weight tends to fall toward the center of the earth by the shortest way." He studied the action of levers, screws, and gears and put some of these studies to use in inventions of many sorts—a lens grinder, a novel spinning machine, mechanical looms, and an automatic printing press that could be worked by one man.

There is no portrait or complete description of Leo-

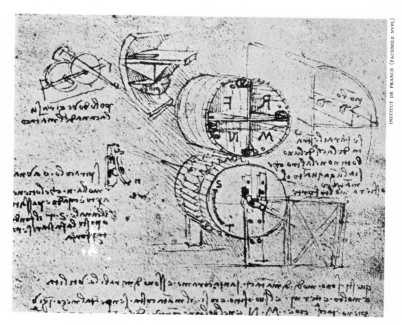

Leonardo made several sketches for the portrait of Isabella d'Este. The drawing opposite may be the final study, since it is pricked for tracing onto canvas. However, the head alone is by Leonardo; a less skilled hand, probably a pupil's, finished the sketch. The only project that Leonardo completed for the d'Este family was the air-cooling machine at right, which was designed for Isabella's sister Beatrice, who was the wife of Lodovico Sforza.

nardo from this time, as he neared his fiftieth year. But according to reports, he dressed carefully and fashionably: he seems to have continued to be as attractive a personality as he was before fame and middle-age came upon him.

Whether in person or by reputation, he succeeded in momentarily attracting the attention of one of the most fascinating men of the Renaissance—Cesare Borgia. This potent nobleman, who was then in his early twenties but had already won triumphs both as a soldier and as a statesman, invited Leonardo to join his military train as his personal architect and chief engineer. Leonardo, perhaps relieved to get further away from painting commissions that had no interest for him, set out to join Cesare's forces in the summer of 1502.

His new patron was at that time finishing a spectacu-

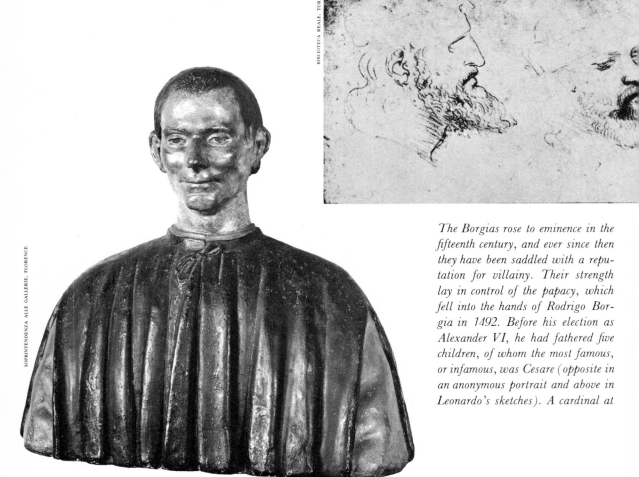

The Borgias rose to eminence in the fifteenth century, and ever since then they have been saddled with a reputation for villainy. Their strength lay in control of the papacy, which fell into the hands of Rodrigo Borgia in 1492. Before his election as Alexander VI, he had fathered five children, of whom the most famous, or infamous, was Cesare (opposite in an anonymous portrait and above in Leonardo's sketches). A cardinal at

larly successful campaign to crush a rebellion against his father, Pope Alexander VI, in the section of northeast Italy known as Romagna. Leonardo's chief task was to inspect fortifications in the newly conquered territory and make suggestions for strengthening them. He also constructed siege engines for his new employer, visited the town of Piombino, where he made plans for draining the marshes, and designed new fortifications for Cesena. For one of Cesare's captains he drew beautiful, detailed maps of the country around Arezzo; these charts, based upon mathematics rather than mere observation, were the forerunners of modern maps.

And wherever he went he carried a sketchbook, filling its pages with everything that caught his eye—workshops, mills, cannon foundries, rocks, farmworkers, horses and

eighteen, he resigned the office in 1497 for a political career. Later young Cesare successfully crushed a rebellion against his father with a combination of cruelty and guile that made his own name a byword for treachery and blackened the family name. Even so, the Florentine Machiavelli (opposite) saw Cesare as a model statesman and immortalized him in The Prince, *a work that became the political guidebook of the era.*

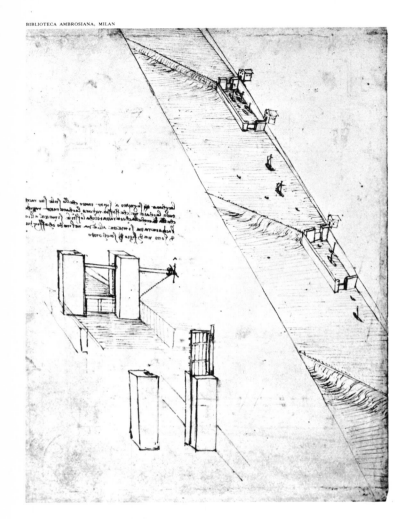

In the midst of his other careers, Leonardo found the time to delve into civil engineering problems. He suggested the first prefabricated houses and city-planning projects. Another idea, to which he returned several times, was the construction of canals and the building of weirs and locks, such as those at left, to make rivers navigable. He also put forward serious plans for creating new fields by draining marsh-

wagons, and laborers in the vineyards. There was no order or special reason in his drawings; he was merely following his own principle of watching and recording. ". . . look to it, O Painter, that when you go into the fields you give your attention to the various objects, and look carefully in turn first at one thing and then at another, making a bundle of different things selected and chosen from among those of less value."

In Cesare's camp, Leonardo became friendly with an important fellow citizen who was there as Florence's special envoy, Niccolò Machiavelli. Machiavelli was a brilliant statesman and was to become the most famous political thinker of the Renaissance. His political treatise, *The Prince*, based on the unscrupulous policies of Cesare

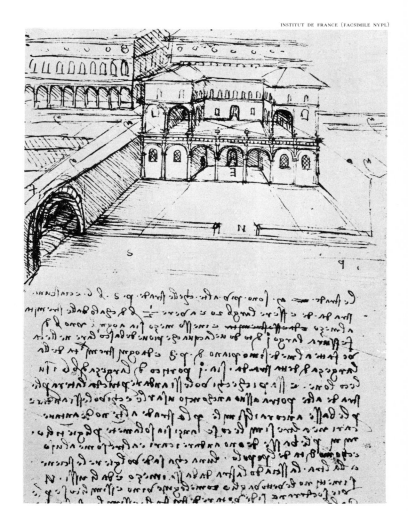

land, and he invented a dredger (above) to dig out the mud. One of his most grandiose and visionary engineering ideas was an imaginary city of underpasses and arcades that is illustrated in his drawing at right. His proposal suggests a solution for modern traffic problems: "The high-level [express] roads are not to be used by wagons . . . all carts . . . should be confined to the low-level roads."

Borgia, whom he greatly admired, was to be the textbook of princes and statesmen for many decades.

But it appears that Leonardo, who hated the savagery of warfare and who was a highly moral man, found less to admire in Cesare than did Machiavelli. Whether because of this, or because the term of his contract had run out, Leonardo returned to Florence—after only ten months' service with Cesare. The occupations he took up in Florence could not, however, be entirely peaceful.

For nine years Florence had been at war with its rebellious vassal city of Pisa. The Pisans were able to defy the Florentine army because ships could bring supplies along the Arno River to the besieged citizens. Leonardo lent his talents to the problem.

69

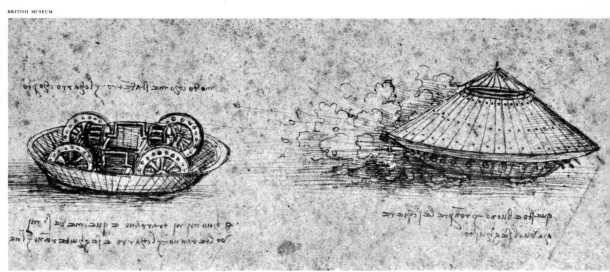

He had studied hydraulics and had written at great length about water and waterways. Now, with the support of his friend Machiavelli, he proposed to defeat the Pisans by diverting the Arno into a canal and cutting off their supply route. But the work took longer and proved far costlier than had been anticipated. When the rainy season began, the workmen all left and could not be coaxed back. The ditches they had dug were filled in by the Pisans, and Leonardo's idea was abandoned.

Leonardo was not discouraged. As an alternative, he devised a prodigious scheme to turn the stretch of the Arno from Florence to Pisa into a navigable canal for peacetime uses. There would be reservoirs to draw on when the river was low, and there would be supporting walls to carry the canal over rivers that had to be crossed. "This will fertilize the country," he wrote enthusiastically, "and Prato, Pistoia, and Pisa, together with Florence, will have a yearly revenue of more than 200,000 ducats . . ." He had even invented a giant earth-mover—an endless chain of buckets worked by a winch and cogwheels—to dig the canal.

Although nothing came of this either, the brilliance of

TEXT CONTINUED ON PAGE 75

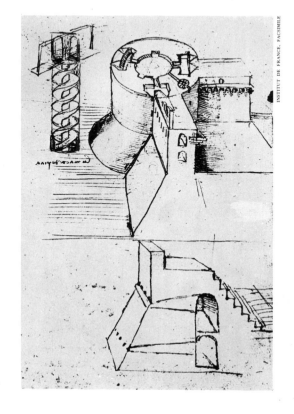

Some of Leonardo's military inventions were as forward looking as his civil engineering ideas. His plan for a tank (opposite at bottom) was practical enough to guide the modern craftsmen who made the model at top (although an actual tank did not appear on the battlefield until World War I). The sloping circular sides of Leonardo's tank were a clever shield against enemy artillery; he used them again in his plan for the fortress at right. The low rounded tower and angled wall became basic principles of fortification in the age of cannon. Leonardo's double-spiral staircase, shown in the skeleton drawing at right, was another new idea; with one-way traffic on each spiral, soldiers could move up and down at the same time.

INSTITUT DE FRANCE. FACSIMILE

DESIGNS FOR THE FUTURE

As far as his scientific research and his mechanical inventions are concerned, Leonardo remained for centuries a prophet without honor. None of his notebooks were published until hundreds of years after his death; only in recent decades has his work been examined and assessed by scientists. Not all of his ideas were practical, or even possible, but few men have been gifted with Leonardo's insight. His work was often hampered by his lack of formal education, especially in mathematics, but a more serious drawback was his lack of a source of power to operate his machines. Even his brilliant mind could not reach forward to the time of the steam engine and the gasoline motor; he had to be content with the strength of steel springs and men's muscles. Three of his most startling prophecies are shown here, in both his own detailed and workman-like drawings and in the operating models that have been made from them. Opposite at top is Leonardo's automobile, powered by two huge springs and steered by means of a tiller attached to the small wheel in the rear. (Gasoline-powered automobiles did not appear until the eighteen-sixties.) At bottom is his self-propelled ship, which was moved by paddle wheels mounted on crankshafts and turned by relays of men. (The first steam-powered paddle wheeler was launched in America only in 1787.) Finally, below, is Leonardo's machine gun—three sets of cannons, mounted on a frame on the carriage axle so that they could be rotated. As one set was being fired the second was cooling and the third was being reloaded. Much the same principle was employed by Richard Gatling in the machine gun, built in 1861, which bears his name.

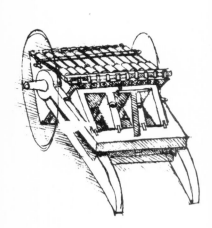

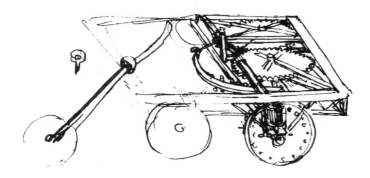

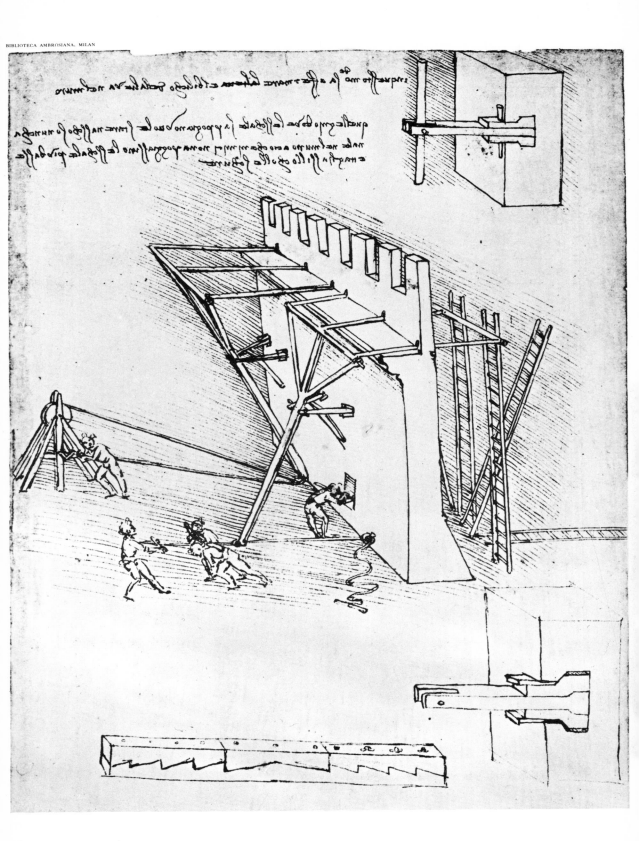

TEXT CONTINUED FROM PAGE 71

Leonardo the engineer was now recognized as equal to that of Leonardo the painter. Florence rejoiced in the greatness of her returned son. Soon after his homecoming, the city council asked him to paint a large mural on one of the walls of the newly built council chamber. Once again, Machiavelli added his support to win the commission for Leonardo; it was the only official work he ever did for his native city.

The theme of the mural was the Battle of Anghiari, in which Francesco Sforza had led the Florentines to victory over the troops of Milan. Leonardo was determined to paint a real battle, one quite different from the stately pageants painted by earlier artists. And in his ten months with Cesare Borgia he had been able to observe the "beastly madness" of war at first hand.

He started by writing a long description of what a battle ought to look like in a painting:

Let the air be full of arrows going in various directions . . . let the balls shot from the guns have a train of smoke following their course . . .

. . . show the mark where a fallen man has been dragged through the dust which has become changed to bloodstained mire, and round about in the half-liquid earth . . . show the marks of the trampling of men and horses who have passed over it.

Make the beaten and conquered pale, with brows raised and knit together and full of the lines of pain . . . show someone using his hand as a shield for his terrified eyes . . . let others be crying out, with their mouths wide open, and fleeing away. Put all sorts of armor lying between the feet of the combatants, such as broken shields, lances, and swords . . . Make the dead, some half buried in dust, others with the dust all mingled with the oozing blood and changing into crimson mud . . . Show others in the death agony grinding their teeth and rolling their eyes, with clenched fists . . .

Leonardo began work on the mural in his usual deliberate way, thinking about the work for months and making a great many sketches in which fiery horses reared or galloped and groups of figures milled about, struggling and fighting. Slowly, his ideas took shape. The action would be centered on an arched bridge at which a fight raged around a battle standard. On one side cavalry would come

When the treasurer of Milan once tried to pay Leonardo with rolls of small coins, the artist refused to accept them because "he was not a painter for farthings." Usually he was paid in florins, named for his native city, where they were first minted, or in ducats, such as the one above (front and obverse). Both coins were made of gold and weighed about 3.5 grams, but their value varied from place to place.

CHASE MANHATTAN BANK MONEY MUSEUM

Some of Leonardo's schemes, such as the defense against siege ladders, opposite, were physically impossible. In spite of this, he recorded them in his notebooks with the same care that he devoted to his useful inventions.

rushing into action, and on the other, soldiers would fight hand to hand. At last, in October, he started a full-sized colored drawing, or cartoon, from which the actual painting would be copied on the wall.

Early in May, 1504, the council, a little nervous at Leonardo's slow, deliberate pace, drew up a new contract. In addition to the thirty-five florins that had already been paid for his materials, Leonardo would receive fifteen florins a month, but the cartoon, at least, had to be finished by February, 1505. For once, Leonardo met the terms of the agreement. He finished the cartoon on time and began to build the scaffold on which he would work.

It was apparent that Leonardo, after his months in the field with Cesare Borgia's forces and after his travails in the

TEXT CONTINUED ON PAGE 80

Uccello's "Rout of San Romano" (above), which is typical of war paintings before Leonardo, looks more like a pageant than a battle. The true violence of combat is better expressed in Leonardo's study for "The Battle of Anghiari" (opposite at top), while the horror-struck attitudes of his men and horses at bottom recall his description of war as "beastly madness."

Peter Paul Rubens knew "The Battle of Anghiari" only through an inferior engraving. Even so, he was so profoundly affected by Leonardo's work that he recreated it in the famous copy at right. The remains of Leonardo's ruined original were destroyed, and replaced with a fresco by Vasari between 1558 and 1565.

TEXT CONTINUED FROM PAGE 76

war against Pisans, was now taking a special delight in the purely artistic problems of composing a great painting for his city. Also, there were reports that the wall of the council hall directly opposite Leonardo's was to be decorated by an ambitious artist named Michelangelo Buonarroti.

A somber and bitter man some twenty-three years younger than Leonardo, Michelangelo had made his reputation first and foremost as a sculptor whose statues were so real they almost breathed. His most recent triumph was a colossal statue of David, carved in marble, which was the wonder of all Florence (see page 143). There was little love lost between the two artists, and whenever they met, harsh words were exchanged. Michelangelo despised Leonardo's fussiness about his appearance and, perhaps, envied his brilliance as a scientist. He was also a devout Catholic, while Leonardo had no religious beliefs. Leonardo had added to the bitterness between them by writing contemptuously of sculpture and poetry, arts in which his rival excelled.

Michelangelo's mural was to show a battle in which Florentine soldiers, bathing in a river, were attacked by the Pisans. This was his first commission for a public painting, and he was determined to make a success of it.

80

However, Michelangelo's mural never went beyond the stage of the cartoon, for early in 1505 he was summoned to Rome by the new pope, Julius II, to design and execute a tomb for him. Yet his finished cartoon, and that of Leonardo, summed up between them, in the words of their fellow artist Cellini, "the school of the world." They were models for the painters who followed them.

Leonardo transferred his drawing to the wall and then began to paint. Almost at once he ran into serious problems. The drying material he had mixed with the plaster darkened his colors and dried too quickly, while a bad linseed oil, sold to him by a dishonest supplier, refused to dry at all and caused some parts of his work to run. However, he managed to finish the central section of the mural, which showed the fight for the battle standard, for a letter written by a visitor in 1549 advises a friend to "take a diligent view of a group of horses (a portion of the battle of Leonardo da Vinci) which will appear a miraculous thing to you."

Once Leonardo realized that his work was ruined, he stopped, and he never returned to it.

However, while he was laboring so unsuccessfully on the battle he was also busy with a portrait, commissioned by a Florentine merchant, which had roused his enthusiasm. It was to be his best-known work, and perhaps the most famous painting in the world.

Michelangelo summed up his creed in one of his own sonnets—for he was no less a poet than an artist: "Nor hath God deigned to show Himself elsewhere More clearly than in human forms sublime." His love of the human figure, influenced by the work of the classical Greek masters, is shown in the copy of his cartoon for "The Battle of Cascina" (opposite). Michelangelo also brought to his work an intense religious feeling, which he expressed in his "Moses" (right). A legend in his own lifetime, after his death his body was smuggled out of Rome, his adopted city, and taken back to his native Florence for burial.

IV INVENTOR

These years that Leonardo spent in Florence were the busiest of his life. He drew up more plans for canals and proposed inventions for draining marshes; he continued his mathematical studies and his work on "The Battle of Anghiari," and at the same time, he was busy with a painting that managed to absorb a great deal of his time and attention. Although he had shrugged off Isabella d'Este's requests for a picture, claiming that he could not stand the sight of a paint brush, he worked quietly away at the portrait of the young wife of a Florentine merchant. She was a beautiful and fashionable lady, with stylishly plucked eyebrows, named Madonna, or Mona, Lisa del Giocondo.

Leonardo painted her sitting serenely with folded hands, looking out at the viewer with the same slight smile that haunted so many of the faces he drew and painted. Behind her is a wild landscape of winding, tortured rivers and craggy mountains that reflects the mystery of the smile while setting off the placid figure.

Vasari described the portrait of Mona Lisa as "an extraordinary example of how art can imitate nature." He wrote: "The eyes possess the moist lustre, [and] the nose . . . the fine nostrils, rosy and tender, as seen in life . . . the mouth, with its red lips, and the scarlet cheeks seem not color but living flesh. To look closely at her throat, you might imagine that the pulse was beating. Indeed we may

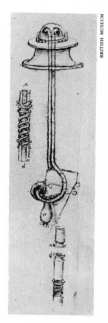

Among Leonardo's many inventions were a number of "machines for water," as he called them, like this diver's snorkel. He abandoned the idea because it might be used for secret attacks on ships in wartime.

Leonardo painted his best-known work, the world-famous "Mona Lisa" (opposite), during his second stay in Florence. Yet, at the time, he had almost given up painting in favor of his scientific research and his inventions.

This striking sketch of rocks may have been a study for the landscape in "Mona Lisa." Leonardo was noted for his realistic backgrounds, which were the result of careful and patient observation.

say that this was painted in a manner to cause the boldest artists to despair."

"Mona Lisa" was a landmark in portrait painting, for Leonardo had breathed life into his subject in a remarkable way. He had created not merely a likeness but a living human being: a true Renaissance portrait that reflected the spirit of humanism—that philosophical interest in man for his own sake (rather than as an art object or as a creation of God) that had sprung up in the intellectual climate of Florence.

Even as Leonardo struggled to express the peculiar character of his subject, he particularly relished the technical problems of painting her, inventing ways of solving questions of composition, of light and shade, of skin tones and textures. He worked at the portrait on and off for three years, probably very much as he had worked at "The Last Supper," leaving it for a long time, then returning suddenly to work on it with renewed interest.

In other paintings that he completed during his second stay in Florence, Leonardo continued to advance toward his ideal of making art imitate nature. He recorded his philosophical theories in his notebooks, intending one day to edit them into a great treatise on painting, and they show the intellectual depth as well as the endless planning and labor that went into all his work.

He thought of art as a special way of looking. It was "the sole imitator of all the visible works of nature." He noted that "the eye . . . the window of the soul, is the chief means whereby the understanding may most fully . . . appreciate the infinite works of nature." To recreate the "works of nature" accurately in his paintings, he studied the world about him, sketching and analyzing what he saw with the objectivity of a scientist. He wrote at great length about the effects of light and shade, the artist's chief tools in creating a solid, real world in his paintings.

He observed how shadows fell: they were sometimes sharp-edged and sometimes fuzzy, and they were not solid black but were made up of lighter or darker shades of color. He noted also that the "part of the atmosphere which lies nearest the level ground is denser than the rest, and that the higher it rises the lighter and more transparent it becomes." In this way Leonardo observed that the bases of mountains seem paler or hazier than their summits and distant things are less clear than near ones.

He studied peoples' gestures and attitudes since, as he said, "action . . . may show what the figure has in mind"; he advised painters to "watch men's postures and actions as they talk, argue, laugh, or scuffle together," and to "make notes of these with a few strokes in a little book which you must always carry with you."

Leonardo realized that the painter's imagination should be constantly at work. He suggested staring at walls spotted with dampness or stains, at clouds, at walls made of different kinds of stones, or at the embers of a fire. These would suggest "figures in quick movement, and strange expressions of faces, and outlandish costumes." (On the next three pages of this book are some of Leonardo's faces, both beautiful and strange.)

The painter should also live alone and choose his companions only from his studio ". . . to obtain the advantages which result from different methods of study." He ought to practice incessantly, study perspective and color, draw every day, and attempt to gather as much knowledge of nature as he could. Leonardo wrote, ". . . as we know, painting embraces and contains within itself all the things which nature produces or which result from the fortuitous actions of men, and in short, whatever can be comprehended by the eyes . . ."

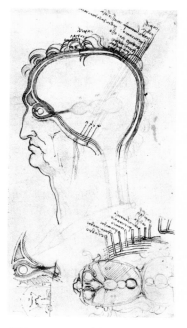

This accurate and detailed drawing of the eye illustrates Leonardo's interest in sight. For him, the eye was a window on nature, and his notes constantly advise the artist to observe the world about him in order to become a better painter.

His passion for research and his respect for knowledge mark Leonardo unmistakably as a man of the Renaissance —and, even more, as a man of Florence. For it was in that rich and thriving Renaissance city, where old ways were being questioned and new ideas were coming into life, that Leonardo's artistic talent had flourished and his philosophical ideas had matured. It was there too that Leonardo's inventive genius began to assert itself. As he probed deeper into the mysteries of nature in order to understand them better as an artist and a thinker, he found he was spending more time on tinkering than on painting. Gradually, he abandoned art for technology and science and became specifically absorbed in a problem that had fascinated him for years—the problem of flight.

From his early youth he had dreamed of flying, and he

was determined to make his dream a reality. Typically, he began by watching closely the flight of birds and then writing down his findings in his notebooks. After studying the structure of birds' wings, he made experiments with models and noted the results. He proposed to gather his observations into a book on the flight of birds. The book would be divided into four parts, the first of which "treats of their flight by beating their wings; the second of flight without beating their wings, and with the help of the wind; the third of flight in general, such as that of birds, bats, fishes, animals, and insects; the last of the mechanism of this movement." He watched the way birds use their tails as rudders and how they make gentle landings by stalling —lowering their tails and spreading the tailfeathers, flapping their wings quickly to cut down their speed, and

TEXT CONTINUED ON PAGE 91

Leonardo's lifelong aim was to combine beauty with scientific accuracy. Many of his sketches for paintings seem diagrammatic, and in his pursuit of the truth, he developed the idea that there was a formula for beauty similar to the mathematical formulas he used as an engineer. Thus began his search for the ideal human face. The four drawings here represent four stages in that search: from left to right they are the Madonna of "The Virgin and Saint Anne" (c. 1488), the angel in "The Virgin of the Rocks" (1483), "Leda" (c. 1505), and a late study of a youth.

LEONARDO'S
"CURIOUS HEADS"

"Leonardo was so delighted when he saw 'curious heads,'" Vasari wrote, "that he would follow about anyone who thus attracted his attention . . . acquiring such a clear idea of him that when he went home he would draw the head as well as if the man had been present." Leonardo's notebooks confirm this statement. They contain several references to freaks and oddities he wanted to remember: "Giovannina, face of fantasy: lives . . . at the hospital. Giuliano da Maria the physician has a steward without hands." Yet he never recorded his "curious faces" in a spirit of mockery: the grotesque monkey-faced woman and the toothless old man at left, along with the strange group opposite, have been portrayed with realism and humanity. Leonardo made no attempt to caricature them or ridicule them. The pain-racked face above at left, bizarre though it is, could be another view of the warrior on the cover. Ugliness was for Leonardo, like beauty, simply one aspect of reality; and, having dedicated himself to the task of mirroring nature in his art, he never flinched at showing the less attractive face of the world.

90

TEXT CONTINUED FROM PAGE 87

changing their center of gravity by moving their heads. He dissected countless birds and bats to learn how the wing opens and closes and how its muscles move it. The end of all of his work was to be an attempt at actual flight.

Others, it happened, had made attempts before Leonardo. One, an Italian mathematician and engineer named Giovanni Danti, had made a short glide over—and into—Lake Trasimeno around 1490; later he made a second attempt at gliding, which resulted in a broken leg. Leonardo was certain he could succeed where Danti had failed.

"A bird," he wrote, "is an instrument working according to mathematical law, which instrument it is within the capacity of man to reproduce . . ." His investigations were spread over a long period of time, during which he watched and studied birds and invented various contraptions that would demonstrate how different surfaces are affected by the movement of air. Among his notes is a drawing of a parachute, made of starched linen, with which, wrote Leonardo, a man would be able "to throw himself down from any great height without sustaining any injury." Another drawing shows a kind of helicopter with a note that a model could be made of pasteboard with a steel-wire spring. "I find that if this instrument . . . be well made . . . and be turned swiftly . . . it will rise high."

His final plan was to build a great bird on which a man could ride, a device lacking, as he wrote, ". . . in nothing except the life of the bird, and this life must needs be supplied from that of man." He knew that a bird's wings were moved by powerful chest muscles. The driving force for the wings of his bird machine, he felt, could be supplied by man's powerful leg muscles, which, he said, were twice as strong as was needed for bearing his weight. He never discovered, unfortunately, that in proportion to its size a bird's bones are much lighter than a man's, and thus he never realized how much power it would take to raise both a man and his machine into the air. He did, however, calculate fairly accurately how large a wing would be needed to support a man in glider flight, and he was far ahead of anyone of his own time—or for centuries to come—in recognizing the effect of air on the surfaces of wings.

Mechanical questions also absorbed Leonardo, among them the problem of flight. Abnormally keen vision and a highly retentive memory enabled him to record the actions of birds in flight in many drawings like the thumbnail sketches above.

BIBLIOTECA REALE, TURIN (FACSIMILE NYPL)

Leonardo's strange drawing opposite—two strikingly different faces confronting each other—may be an analytical study of the good and the evil sides of man's nature. The toothless old man recurs many times in Leonardo's sketches; the youth with the elaborate hairdo may be his pupil Salai.

With particular care he studied the ways in which birds use the wind to rise and descend and their methods of balancing themselves in flight; how hawks rise on air currents, and the way in which they slant their wings and tails so as to take advantage of the wind. He wrote: "The man in a flying machine [has] to be free from the waist upward in order to be able to balance himself as he does in a boat, so that his center of gravity and that of his machine may ... change where necessity requires ..." Many of his notes show his startling powers of vision. He was able to observe, for instance, how a bird prevents itself from being turned over in the air when it is struck from underneath by the wind. He noted that "[the bird] lowers the right or left wing, for this will cause it to turn to the right or left, dropping down in a half circle."

Elsewhere he noted that "when the bird wishes suddenly to turn on one of its sides, it pushes out swiftly, toward its tail, the point of the wing on that side, and since every

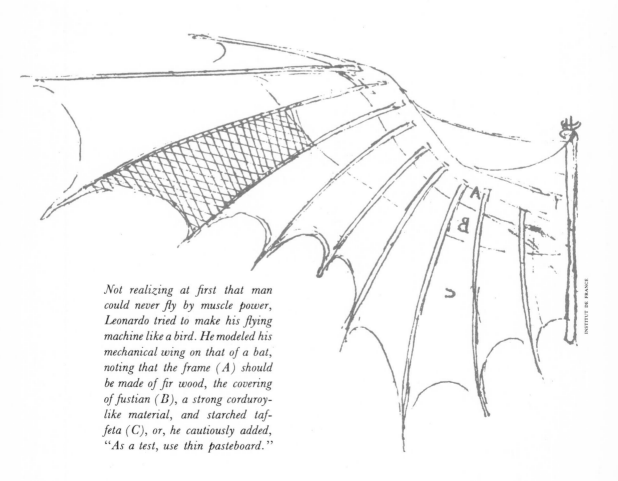

Not realizing at first that man could never fly by muscle power, Leonardo tried to make his flying machine like a bird. He modeled his mechanical wing on that of a bat, noting that the frame (A) should be made of fir wood, the covering of fustian (B), a strong corduroy-like material, and starched taffeta (C), or, he cautiously added, "As a test, use thin pasteboard."

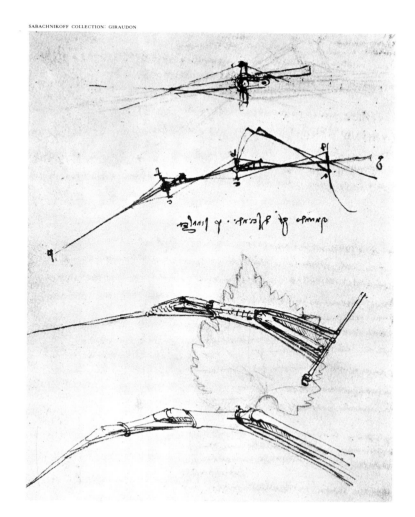

Leonardo made hundreds of studies in order to discover how the bones and muscles of a bird's wing work and how they lift a bird into the air. Two sketches at left below show the strong tendons that open and close the wing, and above them are attempts to duplicate these actions with a system of pulleys.

movement tends to maintain itself, or rather every body that is moved continues to move as long as the impression of the force of its mover is retained in it, therefore the movement of this wing . . . in the direction of the tail . . . will come to move the whole bird with it . . .''

On the basis of such close scrutiny and such precise piecing together of observations, Leonardo built many models, some of them fairly large. He worked on them in great secrecy, for he writes, "Close up with boards the large room above, and make the model large and high, and you will have space upon the roof above . . . if you stand upon the roof at the side of the tower, the men at work upon the cupola will not see you." Later, he made a note to himself to try a small model over the Arno, and he

93

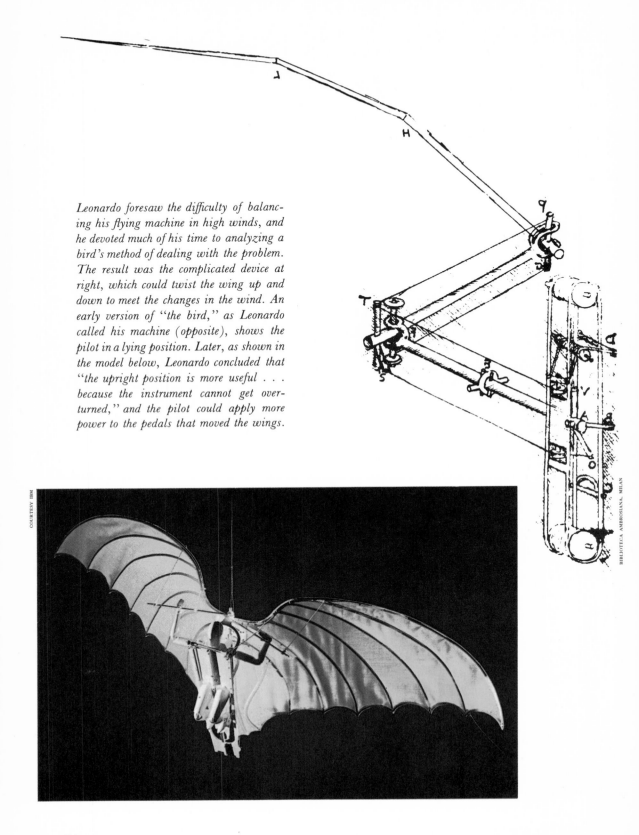

Leonardo foresaw the difficulty of balancing his flying machine in high winds, and he devoted much of his time to analyzing a bird's method of dealing with the problem. The result was the complicated device at right, which could twist the wing up and down to meet the changes in the wind. An early version of "the bird," as Leonardo called his machine (opposite), shows the pilot in a lying position. Later, as shown in the model below, Leonardo concluded that "the upright position is more useful . . . because the instrument cannot get overturned," and the pilot could apply more power to the pedals that moved the wings.

added, "See tomorrow to all these matters and the copies, and then efface the originals and leave them at Florence so that if you lose those that you take with you, the invention will not be lost." He tried all sorts of materials: light fir wood and cane for the framework of the wings, and starched cloth, paper, or parchment for the skin. Joints were padded with leather, springs were made of ox horn or steel wire, and bindings were of strong raw silk.

Leonardo drew plans for several different types of machines. His earliest device had the wings attached to the flier's body. Then, he developed a machine in which the pilot would lie flat on his face, pedaling at stirrups that made the wings rise and fall. Finally, he decided that the best position for the pilot was upright, both because it was more natural and because the machine would then never turn upside down. By this time the "bird" had become very complicated. It consisted of a kind of basket in which the

TEXT CONTINUED ON PAGE 99

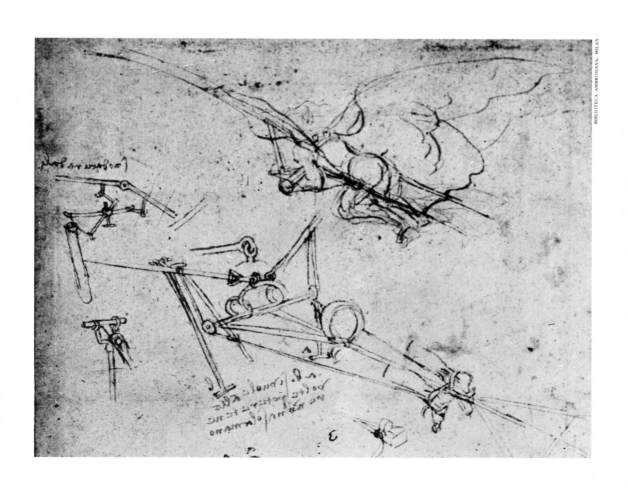

LEONARDO AND FLIGHT

Although Leonardo never abandoned hope that man might fly like a bird—that is, by sailing through the air with wings attached to his body—he also recognized that man might have to find his own peculiar, mechanical means of getting off the ground. Three of the machines he invented for that purpose are shown on these pages: the ornithopter (below) and the helicopter and the parachute (opposite). Of these, the only one wholly impractical was the ornithopter, a flying machine whose four great wings were moved by an operator seated in a bowl-shaped gondola. To make sure the wings cleared the ground, the machine was raised on retractable ladders. Leonardo's helicopter, shown here both in his sketch and in a model, had a screw-shaped rotor operated by four men (to be workable, a powerful engine would, of course, have been necessary). His parachute, though pyramidal, operated in exactly the same way as the modern version; it was to be built of specially treated cloth.

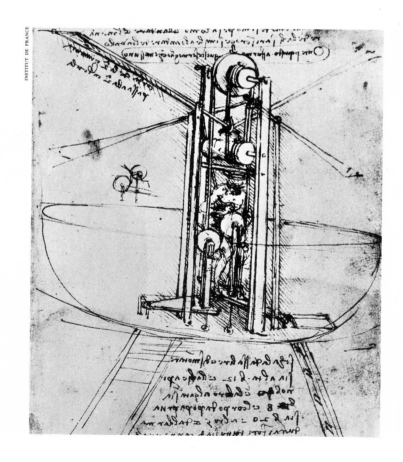

INSTITUT DE FRANCE

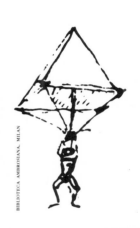

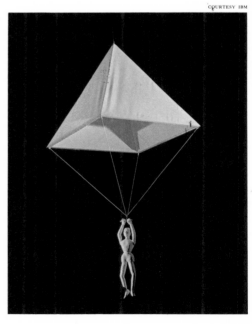

"*From the mountain which takes its name from the great bird, the famous bird will take its flight . . .*" wrote Leonardo. Mount Ceceri (*right*), known as Swan Hill, may have been the scene of his maiden flight. Centuries later, in the eighteen-nineties, the German pioneer Otto Lilienthal (*below*) made a similar trial near Berlin with a machine strangely like Leonardo's.

pilot stood, pumping treadles with his feet, and with his hands turning a windlass to operate two pairs of huge wings. Each pair would move "crosswise after the manner of the gait of the horse." Two long retractable ladders were fastened under the machine to act as legs so that the wings could clear the ground when beating, and Leonardo mentions that some birds such as the martin, or swift, are not able to rise flying from the ground because their legs are so short.

Even while he was still in Milan, Leonardo seems to have tried out one of his inventions, probably a model of a larger machine, for among his records is an entry that speaks of making thongs of oxhide to hold the joints: "Tomorrow morning on the second day of January, 1496, I will make the thong and the attempt."

It is possible that some time in the year 1505 he put his "bird" to the test. Among his papers from about this time there is a page on which is written, "From the mountain which takes its name from the great bird, the famous bird will take its flight, which will fill the world with its great renown." The mountain is believed to be Mount Ceceri, not far from Florence, for the Italian word *cecero* means "swan." This is made surer by a sentence written on the cover of the same notebook: "The great bird will take its first flight upon the back of the great swan, filling the whole world with amazement and filling all records with its fame; and it will bring eternal glory to the nest where it was born."

And then there is silence. No one can say whether the complex machine with four wings was trundled up to a cliff on Mount Ceceri, or whether it was a kind of glider that was tried. Did Leonardo himself make the attempt, or some daring young apprentice? All that is known is summed up in the words of the philosopher and mathematician Geronimo Cardano, writing nearly fifty years later. In his book, *De Subtilitate Rerum*, he remarks, "It has turned out badly for the two who have recently made a trial of it [flying]: Leonardo da Vinci also attempted to fly, but he was not successful."

Not for another four hundred years was man to conquer the air, and then only when a power source, the gasoline engine, had been developed which could give enough power to lift the weight of a man and his "bird"—and only when the principles of lateral balance and steering, first noted by Leonardo, had been rediscovered. Although Leonardo failed, his careful and inventive researches in aerodynamics make him the true forerunner of modern flying.

V   SCIENTIST

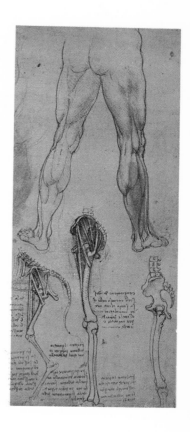

All through his life, Leonardo looked for the truth that lay beneath the outward appearance of the world. He sought for the hidden laws that governed nature. All his studies were directed toward this end. He wrote: "The natural desire of good men is knowledge . . . For as the soul is more worthy than the body, so much are the soul's riches more worthy than those of the body." As he grew older, he became so absorbed with his quest for the cause and meaning of things, with the problem of life itself, that he neglected his painting, which seemed only to be a mirror of nature, the external appearance of life.

More and more he was weighed down by trouble. It seemed that many of his works were failures, and he was oppressed by the passing of time. One line, like a cry of sorrow, appears in his notes: "While I thought that I was learning how to live, I have been learning how to die."

By the spring of 1506, his restlessness and his unhappiness in Florence became unbearable. Nothing went right. His work on "The Battle of Anghiari" was held up until the plaster could be tested further; meanwhile, part of the painting had already been spoiled by his rash use of an experimental drying medium. His experiments in flight had resulted in failure—he never again wrote hopefully of them. He was now fifty-four, and in spite of his years of work and his many achievements, he had no real security. He was

Not content with merely depicting the appearance of nature, as in the sketch of a bramble spray opposite, Leonardo probed beneath the surface in hundreds of anatomical studies like the illustrations of leg structures above.

accused of having deceived the city council by taking its money and not finishing the mural, but his young rival, Michelangelo, who had gone off to Rome leaving only a cartoon, had been paid three thousand ducats for his work. Worries over money were endless, and Leonardo was often humiliated in his attempts to collect what was due him.

Then, at the moment when he was most dissatisfied, most anxious for a change, a letter arrived from Milan that provided the solution to his problems.

After the downfall of Lodovico, Charles d'Amboise, Lord of Chaumont, was appointed governor of Milan. He was already Marshal of France, and Grand Admiral of the French fleet. Chaumont was a man of genuine culture. He had seen Leonardo's model of the great horse, and he had undoubtedly been shown many of his paintings, including "The Last Supper." So, in May, 1506, he invited Leonardo to come to Milan for three months.

Leonardo was ready, but the council of Florence did not want to let him go. The council knew his record of unfinished works, and it feared that "The Battle of Anghiari" would be added to the list. At the end of May, the council drew up a contract in which Leonardo agreed to deposit 150 florins as a bond he would forfeit if he did not return to collect it at the end of three months.

His return to Milan was a triumph. He found Chaumont an intelligent and agreeable employer, and Milan was still a more congenial place in which to work than Florence. In August, Chaumont wrote to the council of Florence asking it to extend Leonardo's leave of absence so that he could finish certain projects he was working on. The council did not like to refuse, since the French had protected Florence from Cesare Borgia, and France did hold enormous power in Italy. But when, in September, Chaumont asked for still another extension, the council wrote angrily, "May your Excellency excuse us from coming to an agreement about the return of Leonardo da Vinci, who . . . has received a good sum of money and has scarcely begun a great work which he is under obligation to finish." Chaumont replied that Leonardo was a very distinguished painter and that in Milan he was held in much esteem. But the council remained firm in demanding his return.

The final decision was made by King Louis XII of France. He was planning another Italian expedition, which would take him through Milan. Knowing this, Chaumont sent the king a painting of a Madonna that Leonardo had recently completed at his request. The king admired it

Charles d'Amboise, Lord of Chaumont and governor of Milan until his death in 1511, was one of the most generous and understanding of all of Leonardo's patrons.

Louis XII was a popular ruler who earned the title of Father of the People. A claim to the throne of Naples through his grandmother led to his invasion of Italy in 1499. He appears here in full armor, setting out in 1507 to reconquer the rebellious city of Genoa, which at that time owed allegiance to France.

enormously. In January, 1507, he summoned the Florentine ambassador and said firmly, "It is time for your council to do me a favor. Write to them that I wish to employ the painter Master Leonardo, who is now in Milan . . ." The ambassador's letter to the council was followed by another, even stronger, letter from the king, and the council dared not refuse. In May, Louis XII arrived in Milan, and Leonardo was confirmed in his position as royal painter and engineer.

The relationship between the Lord of Chaumont and the painter seems to have been a happy one. That com-

"Painting is adorned with infinite possibilities, of which sculpture can make no use," said Leonardo, although he boasted that he practiced "sculpture no less than . . . painting." None of his sculpture remains, but he helped design, and he also supervised, the carving of Rustici's "Saint John Preaching" (below) in the winter of 1507–8.

fortable vineyard and the property outside the city that Il Moro had given Leonardo was restored to him, and for a change he was paid regularly without being constantly harried by his employer. To a certain extent his art suffered, for he painted only a few small Madonnas, "of various dimensions," for Chaumont. Chiefly, he was employed as an engineer, an architect, or as general adviser in matters of art, and apparently this work left him plenty of free time for scientific study. He designed and built some ingenious devices for pageants, as he had done for the court of Il Moro. He planned a wonderful garden, full of fountains, groves, and fish ponds, with hidden jets of water that would spray the passerby, and windmills that would make cool breezes and cause musical instruments to play. These might seem to be the work of a mere toymaker, but for Leonardo they were refreshing diversions from his profound con-

templation of the mysteries of nature. His studies went on.

There was only one interruption to those good days in Milan. The trouble came, as usual, from Florence, and it involved money.

In 1504, Leonardo's father had died without leaving a will, and a furious squabble had started among Ser Piero's other children over the division of the inheritance. Three years later, Leonardo was forced to go to Florence where a lawsuit was pending over Ser Piero's property.

He was received with respect, for he arrived with letters from the king of France urging the council to do everything it could to hasten the judgment. Nevertheless, it was nearly a year before the matter was settled and Leonardo could return to Milan.

There was at least one cheerful side to the Florentine visit. While he was there, he became very friendly with the sculptor Gian Francesco Rustici and spent much time with him. Leonardo enjoyed his company, and in return, gave much help and advice to the sculptor. Rustici had been commissioned to make three bronze figures for the baptistry of the cathedral, and according to Vasari, ". . . they were cast by [Gian] Francesco Rustici but designed and made under the counsel of Leonardo."

During this stay in Florence, Leonardo began to put his notebooks in order, collecting together his observations on botany, mathematics, mechanics, architecture, and many other subjects. But he found the task larger than he could manage at that time, and upon his return to Milan, he

The largest collection of Leonardo's papers is the Codex Atlanticus, so called because of its oceanic size. The codex, compiled by the sculptor Pompeo Leoni, a pupil of Michelangelo's, has 402 pages. Taken to France by Napoleon, it was restored to the Ambrosiana Library, Milan, in 1815. The Codex is kept in the crystal, gold, and lapis box at right, and is labeled "Drawings of machines . . . as well as other things by Leonardo da Vinci, collected by Pompeo Leoni."

BIBLIOTECA AMBROSIANA, MILAN

The chalk cartoon for "The Virgin and Child with Saint Anne" (right) was made in 1499, before Leonardo fled from Milan. But the painting (opposite) was not completed until ten years later, after he had been made official artist to the court of Francis I. Leonardo later took the painting to France and left it to his pupil Melzi, who returned it to Italy after his master's death. A mystery surrounds the work, for in the cartoon, the artist clearly depicted Saint Anne as an older woman, yet in the final version, the mother and the daughter seem to be the same age. Scholars have offered the explanation that Leonardo was unconsciously recreating his childhood, when he had two mothers, his real mother and his stepmother.

abandoned the project. Instead, he plunged even more deeply into his scientific investigations. Now, removed from pressure, and with the support and encouragement of his patron, Leonardo was free to travel, and he could continue his research into geology, in which he speculated on the origin and history of the earth, and anatomy, in which he hoped to probe the very secret of life.

On his many expeditions into the mountains he saw fossil shells—oysters, cockles, mussels, cuttlefish—buried in rock that had once been ocean mud. Since the shells lay not at the tops or on the sides of the mountains but deep within (where they had been exposed by eroding streams), he did not see how the shells could have been deposited there by one great biblical flood. "Here a doubt arises," Leonardo wrote, "and that is as to whether the

Leonardo's influence as an artist spread far beyond the borders of his native Italy. The German master Albrecht Dürer was clearly inspired by Leonardo's early "Adoration of the Kings" (above) when he painted his own version of the subject (opposite) after a visit to Italy. The overall design, the posing of the figures, the ruined setting, and the lighting effects are based on Leonardo; but Dürer went beyond mere emulation when he copied the mysterious rearing horse in Leonardo's background.

Flood which came in the time of Noah was universal or not, and this would seem not to have been the case . . ."

He also began to grasp at the idea of the evolution of species, which even the most distinguished scientists of later centuries could not understand.

His most amazing advances, however, were his anatomical studies. The religious ban on dissecting corpses was rarely enforced by the end of the fifteenth century, and many artists were able to study the construction of the body in the dissecting chamber. Michelangelo and Pollaiuolo had both done so, and as early as 1489 Leonardo had watched doctors performing autopsies. Then he had begun to undertake his own careful dissections. He acquired a set of fine surgical instruments, and as he dis-

TEXT CONTINUED ON PAGE 113

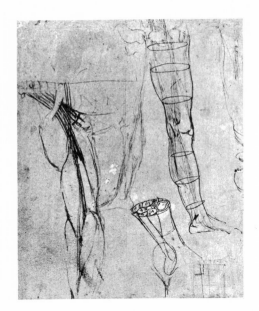

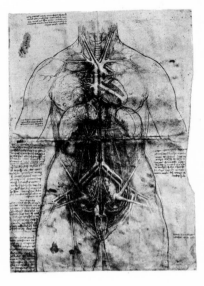

MEN AND MUSCLES

"We shall describe this mechanical structure of man by means of diagrams," wrote Leonardo. But, like so many of his projects, his proposed treatise on anatomy was never finished. Even so, Leonardo raised the study of the "structure of man" to a science. For while most artists of the time were content to portray man's form, he sought to illustrate the inner structure of man: the drawings opposite show the changes in the pectoral muscles as the arm is moved. Though the Church still frowned on the practice of dissecting bodies, Leonardo examined thirty corpses and recorded his findings in hundreds of painstaking diagrams like those above. He tried to give a complete picture of the anatomy by adding cross-section views, such as the one in

the study of leg muscles at upper left. He also invented an original method of illustrating the underlying layers of muscle, tissue, and organs—"transparent" drawings, such as the sketch at lower right showing the internal organs of a woman. His love of mathematics led him to search for proportion in anatomy: his frontispiece for Vitruvius' treatise on architecture (upper right) shows the basic symmetry of the limbs. At last, Leonardo was drawn to study the mystery of life itself. He was the first to dissect the womb and to record it in his tender drawing of an unborn child (lower left). Yet this search too ended in frustration, for he wrote in despair, "Would that . . . I were able to reveal the nature of man . . . even as I describe his figure."

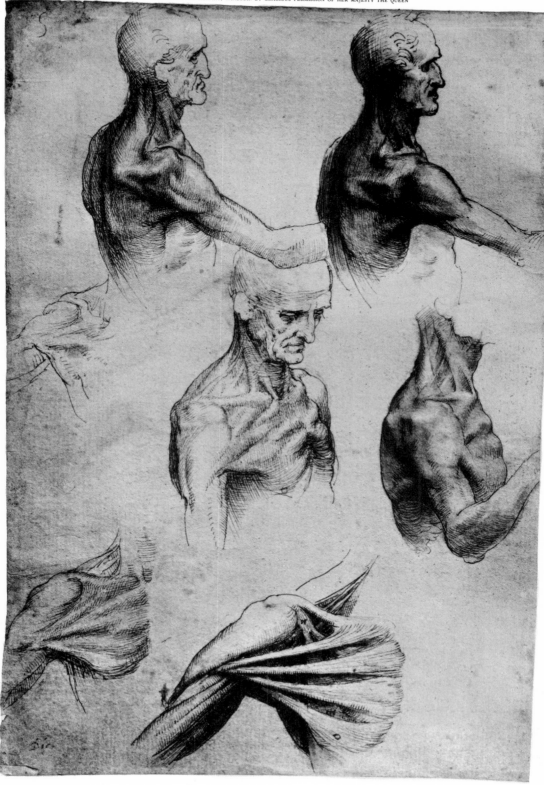

THE ANATOMY OF A FACE

While Leonardo the artist sought for the ideal face, Leonardo the anatomist looked for what lay beneath. He skillfully sliced open the skull to reveal the brain cavity (right) and then the whole bone structure of the face (opposite, at top). Combining art and science yet again, he analyzed the proportions of the head (below) and went on to study the speech organs (opposite, at bottom) and finally speech itself. He reportedly presented his findings, in the form of a treatise on the voice, to Pope Julius II in an effort to win his favor.

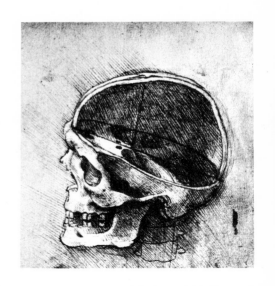

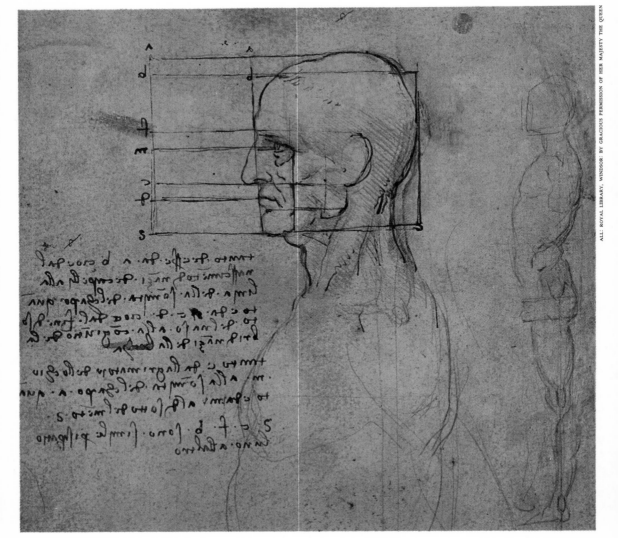

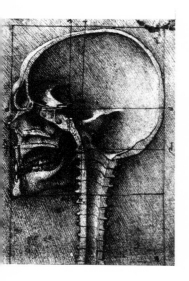

TEXT CONTINUED FROM PAGE 109

sected he carefully sketched everything he saw. At first, he intended to learn about the human body so that he could paint it more realistically. But, as usual, his research became an end in itself, and he began to hope that it would bring him the answer to the riddle of creation. "And would that it might please our Creator," he wrote, "that I were able to reveal the nature of man and his customs even as I describe his figure."

He made hundreds of drawings showing the muscles, the blood vessels, the bones, the various organs of the body, drawings so clear and so accurate that they are still used to illustrate anatomy texts. He tried constantly to find the center of what he called the "vital force," the soul, which gave life to the body. He made experiments on frogs and found that "the frog instantly dies when its spinal cord is pierced; and previous to this it lived without head, without heart . . . or intestines or skin; and here therefore it would seem lies the foundation of movement and life."

But he was not really satisfied with this conclusion. The heart and its network of blood vessels fascinated him, "Marvelous instrument, invented by the supreme Master," he exclaimed. Contrary to most medical opinions of his time, he saw the heart as "a vessel formed of thick muscle, vivified and nourished by the artery and vein, as are the other muscles." He made casts of the aorta—the great artery that carries blood from the heart—by filling the aorta of an ox with wax, making a plaster impression from it, and then blowing glass into the plaster mold. With his glass model of the heart, complete with its valves and compartments, he could study the movement of the blood and its throbbing passage through the body. He also noted that "All the veins and arteries proceed from the heart," and that the beating of the heart produces "a wave of blood in all the veins." In preparing for experiments, he instructed himself to "Follow up the reversive nerves as far as the heart and observe whether these nerves give movement to the heart or whether the heart moves of itself." If its movement came from the nerves, he said, then the soul must have its seat in the brain, where he believed the nerves to originate, while the "vital force" would lie in the left ventricle of the heart. On the other hand, ". . . if this movement of the heart originates in itself, then you will say that the seat of the soul is in the heart and likewise that of the vital powers . . ." It was a problem he was never able to solve completely.

Not content with human dissections, he made many examinations of the bodies of animals, comparing their struc-

TEXT CONTINUED ON PAGE 117

113

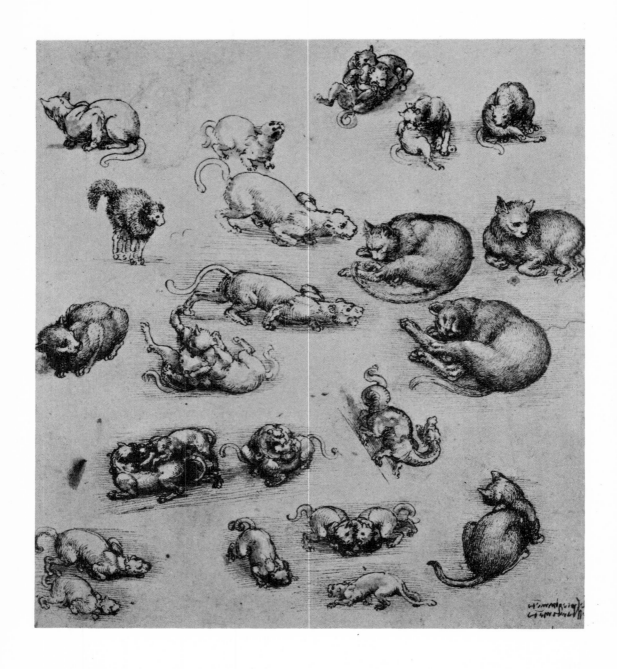

THE STRUCTURE OF LIFE

Leonardo was often impatient with men, but he had a special fondness for animals. Vasari wrote that "he loved all animals and trained them with great kindness and patience. Often, when passing places where birds were sold, he would let them out of their cages and . . . let them fly away." Leonardo was the first anatomist to compare human and animal forms, and he concluded that "as among all the constitutions of the animals [the human body] is of

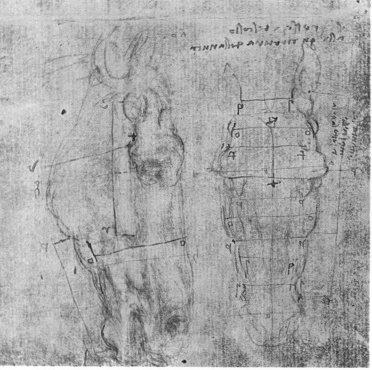

more obtuse and blunt sensibilities . . . an instrument less ingenious and of parts less capable." He analyzed a horse's head (directly above) as carefully as he did a man's. At the same time his lively sketches of cats (opposite) are drawn with great affection, which even extended to monsters: one of the cats has become a dragon (below the slinking cat at center). His notebooks also contain many of the animal fables and riddles that were fash-

ionable in Renaissance Italy, and he intended to publish a bestiary, a half-mythical natural history. The crabs, the dogs, and the bull above were meant to illustrate the stories in that book, in which animals would stand for human virtues and vices. The bull, in Leonardo's words, symbolized "Madness . . . the hunters drape in red the trunk of a tree, and the bull charges it furiously and gets his horns fixed in it and then the huntsmen kill it."

115

TREES AND FLOWERS

Nothing escaped Leonardo's attention, from the solar system to the humblest of plants. And as a botanical artist, his skill was unexcelled: few draftsmen could match the lily or the oak-leaf cluster opposite. Most of his plant drawings, such as the grove of trees at right, above, were drawn for scientific purposes, although many were later used as models for his paintings. The star-of-Bethlehem at right, below, was probably the original of the flower in the lower left corner of the National Gallery's "Virgin of the Rocks" (page 43).

TEXT CONTINUED FROM PAGE 113

ture to that of man, and observing, "In fact, man does not vary from the animals except in what is accidental." He used his technique of wax injection and plaster casting to make delicate models of the brain. He was probably the first to do this, and centuries were to pass before other anatomists were to use the same method to study the brain. One whole notebook is devoted to the growth and development of the human embryo, and his drawing of a child in the womb is perhaps the first of its kind. More than two hundred years after Leonardo's death, Dr. William Hunter, England's first great teacher of anatomy, after seeing Leonardo's sketches, is reported to have said that Leonardo was the best anatomist of his time.

These years spent in Milan, in the service of the French king, were among the happiest of Leonardo's life. He made long journeys, sometimes for pure enjoyment, sometimes on royal business in his capacity as the king's engineer. His notebooks grew and grew as he discovered and sketched and queried everything. Now he would be deep in astronomy, writing, "I must criticize the many ancient writers who state that the sun is no larger than it appears to us." Now he would be in correspondence with the water commissioners on the planning of canals and sluices. He wrote down riddles, philosophical statements, allegories, and curious bits of information about animals taken from ancient bestiaries—some of these seem odd coming from one with so scientific a mind; they are a reminder that he was, after all, a man of the sixteenth century: "The basilisk is so exceedingly cruel that when it cannot kill animals with the venom of its gaze, it turns toward the herbs and plants, and looking fixedly upon them, makes them wither up." Then, again, he writes late at night with all the excitement of the true scientist: "Having for a long time sought to square the angle of two curved sides . . . now in the year 1509, on the eve of the [first day] of May, I have solved the proposition at ten o'clock on the evening of Sunday."

But the good days—and Leonardo's great contributions to the development of the scientific method—were drawing to a close.

Pope Julius II, a great politician and schemer, had formed a league with the German emperor, Spain, and France against the republic of Venice. In 1509, the Lord of Chaumont took to the field, and some of his campaigns may be traced by maps Leonardo made for him. Venice was forced to surrender. When this war was over, Julius II behaved exactly as Il Moro had done earlier: he joined at

The Holy League, formed by Pope Julius II, routed the French armies at the siege of Milan, shown opposite in a painting by Vasari. Giovanni de' Medici (left, center) succeeded Julius as Pope Leo X in 1513; he continued Julius' anti-French policies and finally drove the invaders from Italian soil.

once with his former enemy, Venice, along with the Spaniards and the Swiss, forming a coalition that finally drove the French from Italy.

In February, 1511, Chaumont, governor of Milan, died, and a year later, the French were forced to surrender the city. Massimiliano Sforza, son of Lodovico, entered Milan in state.

Leonardo's very life was in danger. Though a great age, the Renaissance was a time of violence and rapidly shifting fortunes. With no patron, and with his name out of favor at the Sforza court because of his employment by the French, Leonardo found himself cast down from his privileged position. For a time he was able to survive only by moving in with his friends the Melzi family; Francesco Melzi, a boy of twenty, had for years been almost a son to him. Leonardo continued his anatomical studies, but a manuscript page dated January 9, 1513, is written with a blunt pen on coarse paper, and the drawings have a careless look, as though his attention were elsewhere.

In February, 1513, Pope Julius II died of a fever. He was succeeded by Giovanni de' Medici, one of the three sons of Lorenzo the Magnificent. The new pope took the name Leo X, and one of his first acts was to bring his brother, Giuliano, to Rome. Giuliano loved luxury and was a dabbler in philosophy and magic. "He surrounded himself with ingenious men and wished to make trial of every new thing . . ." said a Florentine historian. Like his father, he was known as the Magnificent; in contrast, he was weak and vain and rather foolish. But he was a man who appeared to love both art and science; and Leonardo, the famous artist and scientist, was known to be desperately in need of a new patron. It was decided that Leonardo would go to Rome, and he wrote in his journal, "I departed from Milan for Rome on the twenty-fourth day of September, 1513 . . ."

119

UNIVERSAL MAN

This bird's-eye view of Rome was painted not long before Leonardo's visit there. The Tiber

O n top of the Vatican hill in Rome stands a lovely palace with a magnificent garden and a fine view of the distant plains and hills. It is called the Belvedere. Here, at the beginning of December, 1513, Leonardo moved into rooms prepared for him and set to work. But not, primarily, at painting.

His new patron, Giuliano the Magnificent, was a Medici prince of considerable refinement whose curiosity

River runs across the top of the painting; beyond it are the lordly buildings of the Vatican.

121

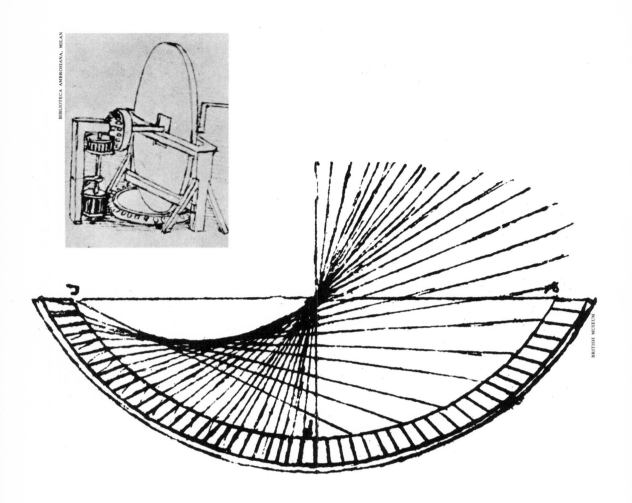

about nature almost equaled Leonardo's. No scientist, Giuliano thought of himself as a philosopher; his interest lay in fanciful devices and novelties, and he was always ready to be pleased by new toys. Leonardo's workshop soon filled with burning glasses and distorting mirrors that he made for his patron. Much of his time was spent building machines so that he could manufacture these curiosities; among them was a massive drawbench that produced strips of copper of uniform size, the first such machine known. At the same time, he made what Vasari calls "an infinite number of follies": hollow figures of animals, for instance, made of a kind of wax paste, which he filled with air. "When he blew into these figures they flew through the air, but when the air within had escaped from them they fell to the earth." Vasari also tells us that "one day the vinedresser of the Belvedere found a very curious lizard, and for this creature Leonardo made wings from the skins of other lizards . . . filled with quicksilver so that

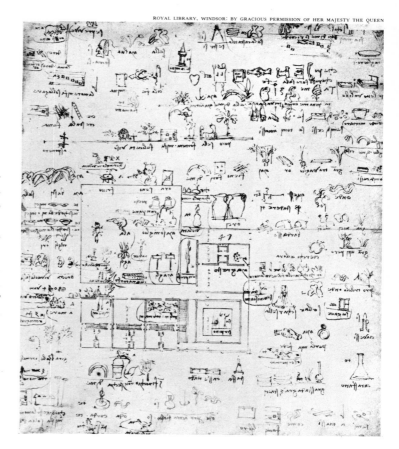

Among the "follies" Leonardo produced in Rome are the designs opposite and above. The elaborately geared machine is a lens grinder: the lens turns at the bottom while being ground by the upright stone. The diagram shows a concave mirror concentrating light at one intense point. The "camera obscura," or projector (above), used a candle as a light source. The doodle sheet at right, one of several such pages penned by the aging artist, appears to be a series of word stories.

when the animal walked the wings moved also, with a trembling motion; he then made eyes, horns, and a beard for the creature, which he tamed and kept in a cage; he would show it to friends who came to visit him, and all who saw it ran away terrified."

He seems to have done little painting, for there are records only of a small Madonna and Child and of an Infant Jesus, which was said to be miraculously graceful and beautiful, but no trace of these remains. And even in this work he was almost more concerned with materials than with the picture. "He made the most singular experiments in seeking oils for painting and varnishes to preserve the work," says Vasari. "It is said that Leonardo, having received a commission for a certain picture from Pope Leo, immediately began to distill oils and herbs for the varnish, whereupon the pope remarked, 'Alas! he will never do anything, for he commences by thinking about the end before the beginning of work.'"

TEXT CONTINUED ON PAGE 126

LEONARDO IN ROME

The festive joust pictured in the engraving opposite is taking place in the court-yard of the Belvedere, where Leonardo had his rooms. But neither such enter-tainments nor the extraordinary architectural activity that was then going on in Rome interested the great master. The job of continuing the rebuilding of the Basilica of St. Peter went to a succession of younger artists—among them Mi-chelangelo and Raphael, who is known to have borrowed freely from Leonar-do's ideas. In the lower scene on the opposite page, Michelangelo is seen pre-senting the final model for St. Peter's to the pope in 1547. The anonymous sketch below, made sometime after the middle of the sixteenth century, shows the con-struction of the circular walls that were to support Michelangelo's great dome.

125

Leonardo found little to encourage him in Rome. The leading artists of Italy had crowded into the city to clamor for work and attention. Rome, long Christianity's spiritual center, had become, under the ambitious popes of the Renaissance, the focus of the world's pomp and glory. Michelangelo, the bitter rival of Leonardo, was the darling of the Romans since he had completed his magnificent paintings for the roof of the Sistine Chapel. Young Raphael was at the height of his popularity. Leonardo, who had always disliked crowds, and who had no desire to compete with younger artists, felt old and tired and neglected.

Personal problems beset him on every side. His health began to fail; there was trouble in his studio where one of the hired craftsmen was neglecting Leonardo's projects to work for other masters. When Leonardo complained, a friend of the craftsman spitefully reported Leonardo's anatomical dissections to the pope, who ordered them to be stopped.

Leonardo wrote a sad letter to his patron, Giuliano, explaining that the completion of his tasks had been delayed by the dishonest craftsman. But Giuliano, though magnificent and a Medici, was not all powerful. He had recently left Rome for Savoy to arrange a political marriage; on his return he had contracted a fever and now lay fatally ill at Fiesole. Shortly before, on the day of Giuliano's departure, Leonardo had received mournful news of the death of his old patron, Louis XII of France.

In despair, Leonardo turned back to research. Always fascinated by water, he began to make drawings and notes for what he may have intended to be a huge painting of the Flood. He plunged into his descriptions with a certain relish, as if already seeing mankind swept away and destroyed. He wrote about it as though it were already happening:

The air was dark from the heavy rain which was falling slantwise, bent by the crosscurrent of the winds . . . It was tinged by the color of the fire produced by the thunderbolts wherewith the clouds were rent and torn asunder, the flashes from which smote and tore open the vast waters of the flooded valleys, and as these lay open there were revealed [in] their depths the bowed tops of trees . . . there might be seen huddled together on the tops of

The dramatic terrors of a rainstorm fascinated Leonardo. His chalk drawing opposite, made before his stay in Rome, shows a peaceful Alpine valley about to be inundated by a frightful storm churning above the mountains.

many of the mountains many different sorts of animals . . . sub-
dued at last to a state of tameness, in company with men and
women who had fled there with their children. And the fields
which were covered with water had their waves covered over in
great part with tables, bedsteads, boats, and various other kinds
of rafts, improvised through necessity and fear of death, upon
which were men and women with their children, massed together
and uttering various cries and lamentations, dismayed by the
fury of the winds which were causing the waters to roll over and
over . . . bearing with them the bodies of the drowned . . .

The sketches that accompany these descriptions are full
of movement, with sweeping, rolling, twisting columns of

water, mountains falling, whirlpools, cities toppling. And on one of the sheets, which shows water swirling around columns, there is a sketch of an old man seated upon a rock with his chin resting on his staff. Nearly toothless, with deep-set eyes, he is the image of care and sorrow. Earlier, Leonardo had done a large self-portrait. Sad eyes peer out from the brows (see page 139). A silky beard falls over his chest, mingling with his long, wavy hair, which is thinning on top. The firm mouth is a little sunken with age. The portrait is full of dignity and power, and yet there is a resemblance to the lonely old man in the little drawing who may be Leonardo himself, weighed down with his images of the end of the world.

He did not paint the Deluge. However, some time during this period he finished what may be his last surviving picture, a painting of Saint John the Baptist. It is profoundly different from other pictures of Saint John—from that drawing of Pollaiuolo's, for example, in which the Baptist is rough, shaggy, and bony. This Saint John is, instead, so handsome that he is almost girlish. He points upward, and Leonardo has given him the same mysterious half-smile that appears in so many of his paintings. However, it is a broader, stronger smile, the smile of a young man full of humor and affection. It shows that Leonardo, though aging and depressed, could not forget his youthful image of beauty.

In March, 1516, Giuliano the Magnificent finally died

The final stage of Leonardo's vision of destruction (opposite) is a maelstrom of water, masonry, and doomed cities. Watching the water patterns at right is an old man believed to be Leonardo himself.

130

John the Baptist was traditionally depicted as a shaggy hermit. In Pollaiuolo's sketch at right, and in the Gospel of Saint Mark, he is "clothed in camel's hair . . . with a girdle of skin about his loins." Leonardo, for reasons not fully explained, broke with the tradition when he painted his "John the Baptist," opposite. His portrait, with its half-smile and mysterious gesturing finger, looks more like one of the pagan gods of antiquity.

at Fiesole. With him died Leonardo's hopes of advancement in Rome. Fortunately, before the year was over, an invitation arrived from France, from the new king, Francis I, who had succeeded to the throne in January, 1515. Leonardo decided to accept, and he prepared to leave Rome. He must have remembered how he had set out long before from Florence with a silver lyre shaped like a horse's skull and a letter from Lorenzo de' Medici. Now, he was leaving another Medici, Pope Leo, to make his last journey. He wrote in his journal the brief, bitter comment: "The Medici created and destroyed me."

King Francis I was a true monarch of the Renaissance. In politics, he was vigorous and subtle, thinking always of strengthening the power of the throne. But he was deeply interested in literature and the arts. Even more than the Italian princes, the Medicis or the Sforzas, who loved display, he saw behind surface glitter and understood

TEXT CONTINUED ON PAGE 135

131

THE IDEAL PATRON

As Leonardo was the universal man of the arts, so Francis I, the king of France, was the universal man among the statesmen of his time. A wise and bold ruler, he was also a generous patron of art, literature, and learning. In the painting opposite, he is shown at center, listening intently while a scholar reads aloud his translation of one of the classical Greek historians. Francis' art collection was unrivaled: it contained treasures like the golden saltcellar above, which Francis commissioned from Cellini about 1540. Architecture too flourished under this cultivated monarch, and the lovely château at Chambord (below) was his favorite building project. It was fitting that Leonardo, Francis' counterpart among Renaissance artists, found his final home in this enlightened court.

*While in the employ of Francis I, Leonardo did a number of costume sketches,
such as this one of a youth with a lance, for the maskers of the king's court.*

Leonardo spent his last years at Cloux. The manor where he lived, and his room with its ornate bed, are seen in the photographs above.

TEXT CONTINUED FROM PAGE 131

what artists were trying to do. He founded the Collège de France, for the study of languages and science, and he was as much the friend of scholars and artists as he was their patron. His court was luxurious: never were there seen such dances, balls, elaborate masques, and gorgeous tournaments. His castles were filled with masterpieces of painting and sculpture, which are today the glories of the Louvre and many other French museums. Above all, he knew that artists must be left to their own devices. Benvenuto Cellini, the famous goldsmith, who entered the king's service in 1540, made clear how delightful this kind of relationship could be when he wrote, "I know not whether the pleasure be greater for the prince who finds a man after his own heart, or for the artist who finds a prince willing to furnish him with the means of carrying on his work." Leonardo was to find King Francis just such a sympathetic patron.

Leonardo was given the small manor house of Cloux, near the king's own favorite château at Amboise. Here, in the green, lovely valley of the Loire, he could relax at last. Francis demanded nothing of him except his conversation, and visited him often. Twenty years later Cellini reported the king as saying "that he did believe no other man had

135

Rising above the Loire River and the roofs of houses in the town, the château of Amboise was begun by King Charles VIII in 1492. It was finished by Francis I shortly before Leonardo arrived in 1516.

been born who knew as much as Leonardo, and this not only in matters concerning sculpture, painting, and architecture, but because he was a very great philosopher." Leonardo was not lonely, nor was he pressed to work, and he was paid seven hundred gold pieces a year. It must have seemed, after the frustrating years in Rome, like heaven.

His daily life was simple, following the rules he had copied down for himself long before: "If you would keep healthy, follow this regimen: do not eat unless you feel inclined, and sup lightly; chew well, and let what you take be well cooked and simple. He who takes medicine does himself harm; do not give way to anger and avoid close air; hold yourself upright when you rise from table and do not let yourself sleep at midday. Be temperate with wine, take a little frequently, but not at other than the proper mealtimes, nor on an empty stomach . . . Rest your head and keep your mind cheerful; shun wantonness, and pay attention to diet."

With the king he outlined several engineering projects of the sort that had always been close to his heart. He proposed to build a canal joining the Loire River and the Cher. ". . . [this] would enrich the lands that it irrigated," he wrote on a sketch map showing one such branch, "and make the country fertile so that it would supply food for the inhabitants, and it would also serve as a navigable canal for purposes of commerce." Along with this scheme go proposals for a walled town with a river flowing through it that would be kept swift and clear, with water wheels to supply fountains in a number of open squares. He made sketches for hunting lodges and palaces, and also for a village of prefabricated houses. "Let the houses," he wrote, ". . . be arranged in order, and this can be done with ease because these houses are first made in parts upon the open places, and are then fitted together with their timbers on the spot where they are to remain." Though these plans were never carried out, it is likely that Leonardo's counsel to King Francis greatly influenced the noble architecture that was then being built in France.

Adviser, consultant, tireless sketcher, Leonardo could not bring himself to make the major effort of creation. His right hand, which had perhaps been injured in earlier years, became arthritic and plagued him. His great intel-

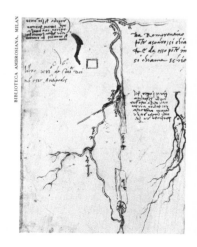

The sketch above is for one of the many engineering projects Leonardo drafted for Francis I: the diagonal line is his proposed canal between the Cher and the Loire. Leonardo's artistic talents were utilized too, but mainly for the staging of mock battles and elaborate tournaments like the one at right.

lect, constantly probing, turned away from the study of nature's mysteries to an inner question: "Tell me if anything at all was done" is a plea that occurs in his notebooks at this time. He could not see what he had actually accomplished. Compared with the other artists of his time, his paintings were few, and many of them had been left unfinished. His great horse had been destroyed. His scientific research was known only to his close friends, for he had published nothing, nor was he able to put his notes in order.

Yet, although Leonardo was unaware of it, his life had had a profound effect on his time. He had stood forth even in that great age of wide-ranging intellect as the universal man, passionately interested in all aspects of existence. He had taught his contemporaries not only a new way to paint but an entirely new way of thinking about art. By combining insight and science with art, by showing his contemporaries that they must observe nature and try to understand it before they painted it, he had led them into a new world, a modern world.

His task was done. Indeed, there were no paintings undertaken during his autumnal years in France, or any great schemes for sculptural projects, or any new scientific studies. The one notable work was a marvelous design for a masque with which Francis entertained his court. The king himself took part in the pageant that Leonardo conceived. Leonardo constructed a great lion that advanced on the king and raised its paws as if about to attack him. But an old hermit—perhaps Leonardo himself—gave the king a magical staff with which he struck the lion. At once, its body opened, showing a great bank of lilies, the flower of France, against a dark blue background. Everyone applauded Leonardo's skill and ingenuity.

In the autumn of 1517, the Cardinal of Aragon, who was touring Europe, came to Amboise and visited the famous old artist in his manor house. An account of this visit was written down by the cardinal's secretary, Antonio de' Beatis, who wrote:

On the tenth of October, 1517, Monsignor and the rest of us went to see, in one of the outlying parts of Amboise, Messer

Though Leonardo's right hand was partially paralyzed in the last years of his life, he could both write and draw with his left hand equally well. The sketch above shows a quill held in his left hand; the signature, like most of his writing, should be read from right to left. Opposite is Leonardo's most famous self-portrait, a brooding study of a giant heavy with years.

Leonardo Vinci the Florentine, an old man of more than seventy years, the most excellent painter of our time, who showed his Eminence three pictures, one of a certain Florentine lady painted from life at the instance of the late Magnificent, Giuliano de' Medici, another of Saint John the Baptist as a youth, and one of the Madonna and the Child in the lap of Saint Anne, all most perfect, and from whom, since he was then subject to a certain paralysis of the right hand, one could not expect any more good work. He has given good instruction to a Milanese pupil who works very well. And although the aforesaid Messer Leonardo cannot color with the same sweetness as he used to, he is still able to make drawings and to teach the others. This gentleman has written of anatomy with much detail, showing by illustrations the limbs, muscles, nerves, veins, ligaments, intestines, and whatever else there is to discuss in the bodies of men and women of all ages. He has also written of the nature of water, of various machines, and of other matters, which he has set down in an infinite number of volumes, all in the common tongue, which if they should be published will be profitable and very enjoyable.

It is a vivid picture of Leonardo in these last years, a portrait from life, despite a few small errors. The fact that Leonardo's right hand was paralyzed would not necessarily have stopped him from further work since he was ambidextrous. The Milanese pupil spoken of was Francesco de' Melzi, who had accompanied Leonardo to France.

How "profitable and very enjoyable" Leonardo's notebooks proved to be, in fact, we know today, for most of

After Leonardo's death in 1519, his body was buried in a church in the town of Amboise outside the walls of the château, which are visible in the engraving below. But after the French Revolution, when much of Amboise was destroyed, remains thought to be his were reinterred in St. Hubert's Chapel (opposite), which may be found in the engraving next to the word "Amboise."

them had to wait nearly four hundred years for their publication. And they are an unfailing source of information on what Leonardo was creating and what he was thinking. The man who once planned war machines more terrible than any dreamed of in his time now gave his attention to mock battles in which make-believe forts were built of cloth, and guns fired hollow cannonballs made of papier-mâché. Though perhaps frustrated by the lack of serious accomplishment, and though ailing, he was, nonetheless, content to remain where he was—in the most brilliant court in Europe. On one page of paper he wrote, in a hand still firm and clear, "On the twenty-fourth of June, St. John's Day, 1518, at Amboise in the palace of Cloux," and below it, "I will go on."

The summer passed and was followed by a bitter winter. In the spring, Leonardo sent for the royal notary to come and take down his last will and testament. In it,

TEXT CONTINUED ON PAGE 144

AFTER LEONARDO

Raphael and Michelangelo were the direct heirs of Leonardo. Differing widely from each other, and from Leonardo, in temperament and outlook, each in his own unique way carried on Leonardo's work. Raphael continued the quest for ideal beauty. He followed Leonardo closely in style, in form, and even in the composition of his paintings. His "Holy Family" (above) might well have been taken directly from the earlier cartoon of "The Virgin and Saint Anne" (page 107): the grouping of the figures, the landscape, the wrinkled face of Saint Anne, even the traveling basket at her feet, all seem to have been copied from Leonardo's drawing. Michelangelo, however, struck out in a new direction.

From Leonardo he learned to observe nature, but he added to his work a fierce intensity that mirrored not only his own stormy nature but the disordered state of an Italy that had fallen to foreign conquest. This trait, which his contemporaries called *terribilità* (the power to inspire awe and terror), was expressed in massive, heroic works such as his eighteen-foot-high "David" (opposite), hewn from a marble block abandoned by another sculptor. Both of these great artists, then, and the men who succeeded them either in the search for classical beauty or in the attempt to express man's spirit in art, followed paths that had been indicated by the son of Ser Piero, the notary of Vinci.

142

143

LEONARDO'S GENIUS
APPRAISED BY CRITICS THROUGH THE AGES

Wherefore nature favored him so greatly that in whatever his brain or mind took up, he displayed unrivaled harmony, vigor, vivacity, excellence, beauty, and grace. His knowledge of art, indeed, prevented him from finishing many things which he had begun, for he felt that his hand would be unable to realize the perfect creations of his imagination . . .

GIORGIO VASARI
Italian painter, sculptor, art historian
Life of Leonardo da Vinci, 1558

Leonardo da Vinci began by examining each object in the light of an exact theory and then proceeded to explain it against the natural background that he wanted to use. . . . He knew how to impart to each thing the liveliest, the most specific and convenient character and could enhance the concept of majesty to the point of making it divine.

PETER PAUL RUBENS
Flemish painter
in R. de Piles *Summary of the Life of Painters*, 1699

Thanks to this method [using light and shade in his paintings] he reproduced, in his wonderful faces and figures, all that nature itself can do. And in this he was superior to all, so that one may safely claim that Leonardo's lights were divine.

G. P. LOMAZZO
Italian art historian
The Idea of the Temple of Painting, 1590

The many gifts bestowed upon him by nature were embodied mainly in his eyes; though he was a universal genius, Leonardo was first and foremost a great painter. Regularly and perfectly formed, he appeared, next to common humanity, as an ideal specimen of it. Just as clarity and perception of sight are generally referred to the intelligence, so clarity and intelligence were typical of him.

JOHANN WOLFGANG VON GOETHE
German poet
Art and Antiquity, 1817

TEXT CONTINUED FROM PAGE 141

he left all his notebooks and "other instruments and portraits connected with his art and occupation of painter" to Francesco de' Melzi. To Melzi, also, he left all his ready money and all payments due to him. To his brothers in Florence he left four hundred ducats. To his servant, Giacomo Salai, who had been with him for more than twenty years, he left half of his vineyard at Milan; the other half was left to another faithful servant, Battista de Villanis. He arranged for his own funeral services, in careful detail, down to the weight of the candles to be burned. Then he resigned himself to wait for death.

It was not long in coming. Seven days after he had made his will, on the second of May, 1519, Leonardo died. He was buried quietly in a church at Amboise, and some

Leonardo is *par excellence* the painter of mystery, of the ineffable, of dusk; his pictures appear as music in a minor key. His shadows are veils through which he leaves an opening, or which he thickens to let us guess at a secret thought.

THÉOPHILE GAUTIER
French writer and critic
Italian Journey, 1875

We forget that genius means mental energy, and that a Leonardo, for the self-same reason that prevents his being merely a painter—the fact that it does not exhaust a hundredth part of energy—will, when he does turn to painting, bring to bear a power of seeing, feeling, and rendering . . . utterly above that of the ordinary painter . . . No, let us not join in the reproaches made to Leonardo for having painted so little; because he had much more to do than to paint, he has left all of us heirs to one or two of the supremest works of art ever created.

BERNARD BERENSON
American art critic
The Italian Painters of the Renaissance, 1896

Perhaps the world knows of no other example of a genius so universal, so endowed with imagination, so unsatisfiable, so thirsting for the eternal, so naturally subtle, so pushed forward beyond his own century and the centuries to come. His figures express incredible spirit and sensitivity; they are spilling over with ideas and unexpressed feeling.

HIPPOLYTE TAINE
French philosopher and art historian
Italian Journey, 1897

From the first he is obsessed by vital force and finds it expressed in plants and creatures; then, as his scientific researches develop he learns the vast power of natural forces, and he pursues science as a means by which these forces can be harnessed for human advantage. The further he penetrates the more he becomes aware of man's impotence . . . human beings cease to be the center of nature; so they gradually fade from his imagination, or when they appear, as Saint Anne or Saint John, they are human no longer but symbols of force and mystery, messengers from a world which Leonardo da Vinci, the disciple of experience, has not explored, though he has earned the right to proclaim its existence.

SIR KENNETH CLARK
English art historian
Leonardo da Vinci, 1939

days later Melzi brought the news of his passing to King Francis, who was then at the castle of St.-Germain-en-Laye. A royal historian wrote, "Francis, king of France, wept in sorrow when Melzi told him that [Leonardo] was dead." A month later, Melzi wrote to Leonardo's brothers, giving them the news. "To me he was like the best of fathers," he said. "It is a hurt to anyone to lose such a man, for nature cannot again produce his like."

Centuries later, the church at Amboise was wrecked during the French Revolution. A gardener collected whatever fragments he could find and buried them all together in one grave. Then, somewhat later, near the end of the nineteenth century, the French poet and critic Arsène Houssaye, digging on that spot, found what he believed was Leonardo's skull and some of his bones. These lie today in the little chapel of St. Hubert, in Amboise château, and above them is an inscription that says: "Under this stone lie bones gathered in the excavations of the ancient royal chapel of Amboise, among which it is thought there are the mortal remains of Leonardo da Vinci."

Thus, the mortal remains of Leonardo are contested, much as many of the works attributed to him are debated. And the Italian Renaissance itself, that great advance of the human spirit to which Leonardo contributed so much,

Neither the mountains of northern Italy (shown here in a drawing by Leonardo on red paper) nor the end of the Italian Renaissance prevented the spread of Leonardo's ideas into other lands and other times.

ended violently only a few years after his death—in 1527 when the forces of Emperor Charles V sacked Rome.

But the enlightenment of the Renaissance was by no means restricted to Italy. Even before Leonardo's departure for France, it was abroad, spreading throughout the countries of Europe and to distant lands that were even then being colonized overseas. And as it spread, it awakened new generations to continue the search that Leonardo had begun, the artistic and scientific search for the true picture of man and his universe.

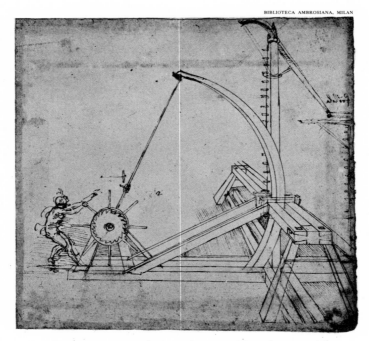

BIBLIOTECA AMBROSIANA, MILAN

One of Leonardo's many drawings of war machines shows a soldier attempting to bend back the arm of a sling by means of a ratcheted wheel.

AMERICAN HERITAGE
PUBLISHING CO., INC.

James Parton, *President*

Joseph J. Thorndike, Jr., *Editor in Chief*

Richard M. Ketchum, *Editorial Director, Book Division*

Irwin Glusker, *Art Director*

HORIZON CARAVEL BOOKS

RUSSELL BOURNE, *Editor*

Sean Morrison, *Assistant Editor*

Janet Czarnetzki, *Art Director*

Susan H. Griggs, *Picture Researcher*

Elaine K. Andrews, *Copy Editor*

Nancy Simon, *Editorial Researcher*

Betsy Sanders, *Editorial Assistant*

Gertrudis Feliu, *Chief, European Bureau*

ACKNOWLEDGMENTS

The Editors would like to express their appreciation to the staff members of the private and public collections in Europe and the United States where the paintings, drawings, and items of particular importance to this book were found. Special thanks are owed to Susanne Puddefoot in England and to Maria Todorow and Fiorella Ginanneschi in Italy for their assistance, and to the following individuals and organizations for their generous cooperation.

Miss A. H. Scott-Elliot, Royal Library, Windsor Castle
Biblioteca Ambrosiana, Milan
Department of Prints and Drawings, British Museum
Dorothy Bishop, IBM Gallery, New York
Cabinet des Estampes, Bibliothèque Nationale, Paris
Cabinet des Dessins, Louvre
The Art, Science, and Rare Book divisions of the New York Public Library
National Gallery of Art, Washington

Grateful acknowledgment is made for permission to quote from the following works:

All the Paintings of Leonardo da Vinci. Costantino Baroni. Hawthorn, New York, 1961.

Italian Painters of the Renaissance. Bernard Berenson. (Phaidon) N.Y. Graphic, 1957.

Leonardo da Vinci, Kenneth Clark. Cambridge University Press, 1958.

Leonardo da Vinci. Ludwig Goldscheider. Phaidon Press, London, 7th Edition, 1964.

The Notebooks of Leonardo da Vinci. Trans. by Edward MacCurdy. Braziller, New York, 1958.

FURTHER REFERENCE

Readers interested in viewing additional examples of Renaissance art will find collections in the following museums: The Metropolitan Museum of Art and the Frick Collection in New York City; the National Gallery of Art, Washington, D.C.; the Cleveland Museum of Art; the Museum of Fine Arts of Houston, Texas; and the Seattle Art Museum. The Elmer Belt Library of Vinciana, University of California, has an extensive collection of material on Leonardo.

For those who wish to read further on Leonardo and the Renaissance in Italy and France, the following books are recommended:

Baroni, Costantino, ed. *All the Paintings of Leonardo da Vinci*. Hawthorn, 1961.

Berenson, Bernard. *Italian Painters of the Renaissance*. (Phaidon) N.Y. Graphic, 1957.

Blunt, Anthony. *Artistic Theory in Italy, 1450–1600*. Oxford, 1962.

Burckhardt, Jacob. *The Civilization of the Renaissance in Italy*. 2 vols. (Torchbooks) Harper, 1958.

Cellini, Benvenuto. *The Autobiography.* . . . (Dolphin) Doubleday, 1960.

Clark, Kenneth. *Leonardo da Vinci*. Cambridge University Press, 1958.

Freedberg, S. J. *Painting of the High Renaissance in Rome and Florence*. 2 vols. Harvard University Press, 1961.

Friedenthal, Richard. *Leonardo da Vinci, A Pictorial Biography*. (Studio) Viking, 1959.

Goldscheider, Ludwig. *Leonardo da Vinci*. (Phaidon) N.Y. Graphic, 1964.

Hart, Ivor B. *The Mechanical Investigations of Leonardo da Vinci*. University of California Press, 1963.

Heydenreich, Ludwig Heinrich. *Leonardo da Vinci*. 2 vols. (Holbein) Macmillan, 1955.

Leonardo da Vinci. Exhibition Catalogue. International Business Machines Corporation, 1951.

Lucas-Dubreton, J. *Daily Life in Florence in the Time of the Medici*. Macmillan, 1961.

MacCurdy, Edward. *The Notebooks of Leonardo da Vinci*. Braziller, 1958.

McCarthy, Mary. *The Stones of Florence*. Harcourt, Brace, 1959.

Maurois, André. *An Illustrated History of France*. Bodley Head, 1963.

Pater, Walter. *The Renaissance*. (Mentor) New American Library, 1963.

Plumb, J. H. and the Editors of *Horizon*. *The Horizon Book of the Renaissance*. American Heritage, 1961.

Popham, A. E. *The Drawings of Leonardo da Vinci*. (Harvest) Harcourt, Brace & World, 1945.

Symonds, John Addington. *The Renaissance in Italy*. 2 vols., *The Age of Despots* and *The Revival of Learning*. (Capricorn) Putnam, 1960.

Vasari, Georgio. *Lives of the Artists*. Modern Library, 1959.

For his many studies of draped figures, Leonardo made models and covered them with cloth dipped in clay.

INDEX

Bold face indicates pages on which maps or illustrations appear